The New Pilgrims

John A. Forrester

The New Pilgrims

Reflections on Christian Conversion at the Beginning of the Third Millennium

John A. Forrester

Pastor's Attic

www.pastorsatticpress.com

For

Martin Grove Baptist Church

faithful to their Lord

lovers of his people

welcoming all he brings

boldly marching into his future

under the ancient-modern banner of

CHRISTUS VICTOR

Contents

Prescript

(Nicodemus makes a beginning)

Now there was a man of the Pharisees named Nicodemus, a ruler of the Jews. [2]This man came to Jesus by night and said to him, "Rabbi, we know that you are a teacher come from God, for no one can do these signs that you do unless God is with him." [3]Jesus answered him, "Truly, truly, I say to you, unless one is born again he cannot see the kingdom of God." [4]Nicodemus said to him, "How can a man be born when he is old? Can he enter a second time into his mother's womb and be born?" [5]Jesus answered, "Truly, truly, I say to you, unless one is born of water and the Spirit, he cannot enter the kingdom of God. [6]That which is born of the flesh is flesh, and that which is born of the Spirit is spirit. [7]Do not marvel that I said to you, 'You must be born again.' [8]The wind blows where it wishes, and you hear its sound, but you do not know where it comes from or where it goes. So it is with everyone who is born of the Spirit."

[9]Nicodemus said to him, "How can these things be?" [10]Jesus answered him, "Are you the teacher of Israel and yet you do not understand these things? [11]Truly,

truly, I say to you, we speak of what we know, and bear witness to what we have seen, but you do not receive our testimony. [12]If I have told you earthly things and you do not believe, how can you believe if I tell you heavenly things? [13]No one has ascended into heaven except he who descended from heaven, the Son of Man. [14]And as Moses lifted up the serpent in the wilderness, so must the Son of Man be lifted up, [15]that whoever believes in him may have eternal life.

[16]*"For God so loved the world, that he gave his only Son, that whoever believes in him should not perish but have eternal life. [17]For God did not send his Son into the world to condemn the world, but in order that the world might be saved through him. [18]Whoever believes in him is not condemned, but whoever does not believe is condemned already, because he has not believed in the name of the only Son of God. [19]And this is the judgment: the light has come into the world, and people loved the darkness rather than the light because their works were evil. [20]For everyone who does wicked things hates the light and does not come to the light, lest his works should be exposed. [21]But whoever does what is true comes to the light, so that it may be clearly seen that his works have been carried out in God."*

John 3:1-21[1]

---

[1] All Bible quotations are from the English Standard Version.

Introduction

It is 12:25 on a Sunday afternoon. I am just finishing the round of greetings, catch-ups, and four minute counseling spots after the second worship service. I have an important meeting at 12:30 (not the best of scheduling!) Suddenly Jade,[2] Taiwanese, an energetic and faithful lay leader, comes excitedly towards me. "Pastor, can you talk to this couple? The husband wants to become a Christian." And so I am introduced to Michael Sun and Jenny Li.

I don't recall meeting them before. In a few days they will go back to China for an extended visit to care for Michael's aging mother. Do they know anything about the Christian faith? Have they ever seen a Bible? What is Michael's motive for becoming a Christian? Will there be a church home waiting for him back in China? How good is their English? They seem so young.

And the jailer called for lights and rushed in, and trembling with fear he fell down before Paul and Silas. Then he brought them out and said, "Sirs, what must I do to be saved?"
Acts 16:29-30

---

[2] The names have been changed.

I wonder where to begin. It is now 12:29 on that Sunday afternoon, early in the third millennium, in Vancouver, Canada—post-Christendom, post-modern, post-monocultural, post-Boomer, post-liberal, post-fundamentalist, post the last recognizable landmark. I am the lead pastor and I am supposed to know what to do.

This church is a 90-year-old congregation in a residential area of the city. On one side of the property is the main artery from the airport to the downtown core; on the other side, one of the principle routes out to the university. A couple of decades ago this congregation was primarily middle and upper class white. But the neighbourhood was changing. Property prices soared as new immigrants, primarily from Asia, moved into the area.

The church began to look around nervously. Will we survive this demographic sea-change? Where will the next generation come from? Our children are all moving out to the more affordable suburbs. Should the church follow them, as other churches have? Or is it possible to remain in place and somehow adapt? Where are you leading us Lord?

After much prayer and discussion it seemed good to the leaders of the day for the church to retain the same address and look for ways to embrace this new world. And by the grace of God the church began to change. Of the people who now flock in through the doors on a typical Sunday morning, about 35% are Chinese and 25% Filipino. About 40 nations are represented in the church in total. There is still a core remnant from earlier days with some in their 90's, but the overflowing church now has lots of young families also.

And there are other changes. Many who come through the doors these days do not have even the most basic understanding of the Christian faith, either because they have come from countries with little Christian influence, or because they have grown up here in what is now one of the most secular cities in North America. This church has become an amazing gathering of all kinds of people. It is diverse in multiple directions: culturally, racially, generationally, theologically, socio-economically. And it is also evangelical.

In 1989 David Bebbington, the Scottish theologian and writer, proposed a summary of evangelicalism that has provided a useful starting point for recent discussions.[3] He highlights four features (often called the "Bebbington quadrilateral"): *conversionism*, *activism*, *biblicism*, and *crucicentrism*. His vocabulary is awkward, especially "crucicentrism," by which he means simply that evangelicalism is cross-centred. But his summary is helpful. Evangelicals, he argues, focus on these four areas: conversion, activism, the Bible, and the cross.

It is Bebbington's "conversionism" that is the focus of this essay. What is the nature of Christian conversion at the beginning of the third millennium? Is conversion different now than it was in, say, 1950? It certainly looks different. What does conversion *mean* today?—conversion from *what* to *what*? It appears as though the new social and cultural environment has changed the dynamics of Christian conversion. But neither

---

[3] David W. Bebbington, *Evangelicalism in Modern Britain: A History from the 1730s to the 1980s* (Routledge: 1989).

Christ nor his Gospel has changed, we believe. So what remains and what has changed, if anything?

We as evangelicals desire, under God, to facilitate conversion—or better, to be partners with God in his conversion of men and women. But what does it mean to obey the Great Commission, at this point in history, in a place like Vancouver? It may be helpful to pause and reflect theologically on the nature of our ancient task in this new setting. Have we examined what has been delivered to us from earlier generations?—have we made it our own? Or have we simply followed what was helpful for others in their day, but now needs re-thinking for a new cultural context?

And what about our own conversions? Why are we often reluctant to "give our testimony"? Is it because we are worried our conversion doesn't match our model? (or the model of the authority figures around us?) Is it possible to be set free to value and validate our own personal pilgrimage with God, even if our journey seems suspect to some? What is a *biblical* conversion anyway? It appears that Scripture describes a greater diversity of conversion experience than some church traditions have been willing to embrace. Are we ready to give Scripture a fresh hearing on this matter?

In a 1980 essay, "Conversion as a Complex Experience," Orlando Costas reflects on the complexity of his own conversion. He begins: "Conversion, in the traditional evangelical understanding, is a static, once-for-all, private experience . . . a trans-cultural, non-contextual event . . . ." In contrast to this he argues for conversion as a "dynamic, complex, ongoing experience, profoundly responsive to particular times and places and shaped by the context of those who experience it."[4]

Costas is Latin American by birth. He moved to the U.S. with his family at the age of twelve from Puerto Rico. On June 8, 1957, at a New York Billy Graham Crusade, Costas "went forward." But that was not the first time he had made a public profession of faith. He describes his conversion as a pilgrimage moving through at least three "concentric circles"—to Christ, to culture, and to the world.[5] Costas points to Paul's words to support his contention that conversion is both event and process:

> [16] *But when one turns to the Lord, the veil is removed . . .*
> [18] *And we all, with unveiled face, beholding the glory of the Lord, are being transformed into the same image from one degree of glory to another. For this comes from the Lord who is the Spirit* (2 Cor. 3:16, 18).

Costas helpfully demonstrates the value of open reflection on our own conversion I believe this is vital, especially for those of us in pastoral roles. Our own experience of conversion will shape the contours of both our personal growth and our public ministry. The better we understand our own conversion the better we will understand ourselves. This understanding itself will be a journey. Only in heaven will we fully grasp how deeply and comprehensively God has been at work in us. But there is still work to be done here on earth. And as we revisit our conversion, our present way of being—our *spirituality*—

---

[4] Orlando E. Costas, "Conversion as a Complex Experience—A Personal Case Study" in *Down To Earth: Studies In Christianity and Culture*, eds. Robert T. Coote and John Stott (Grand Rapids, MI: Eerdmans, 1980), p. 173.
    [5] Ibid., p. 176f

will be enriched, and our outflow—our *ministry*—will spring from deeper places, with deeper authenticity. We will own our ministry more fully.

To summarize what is to come in this essay, I begin by highlighting some of the ways in which our (western) world is changing. This is important because I believe it is changing in ways that compel us to ask new questions about conversion. Next I summarize and evaluate the work of four authors who bring fresh thinking to this subject. This then brings me to some proposals for a new agenda for the church, presented as four transitions. I close with four stories illustrating the issues surrounding conversion at the beginning of this third millennium, and some reflections on the Great Commission (Matthew 28:18-20).

If this essay seems brief for the territory covered, my only defense is that it was originally even briefer. It was first written for an audience of one, my professor. In this revised version I have expanded and clarified considerably, and have reduced the content of footnotes to simple citations, where possible. I trust this study will now be helpful to a somewhat wider audience. If it still seems over-compressed at times, suggestions for further reading may be found in the bibliography.

For some readers this will feel like water under the bridge. They are already reasonably comfortable navigating the stiff, new undercurrents and taxing cross-winds of our dramatically changed social environment. But most of us who desire to serve the people of God in these often baffling times can benefit from ongoing reflection. I trust this essay will "stir the pot" in a helpful way, not only stimulating a more thorough exegesis of our present cultural milieu, but also encouraging a deeper confidence in the Lord of the harvest for our time.

And one more note of explanation. The rallying cry of traditional evangelicals has been, "You must be born again." But paradoxically, the conversion of the man Nicodemus, to whom Jesus spoke those words (and the only place where "born again" language is used in the Bible) doesn't appear to fit the traditional evangelical model! I trust that the ambiguous and mysterious spiritual pilgrimage of Nicodemus will provide a thought-provoking backdrop for this study.

1. New Contexts For Conversion

Despite our propensity to resist and deny, our world has changed. We will never again see 1995, let alone 1955. One way to describe this change is as a series of passings. This is not intended as a negative framing of change. It is simply a way to emphasize the "pastness of the past," surely the first step in moving on—specifically, here, in regards to evangelical endeavors focusing on conversion.

a) The Post-Christendom World

Christians of the West are only just beginning to come to terms with the reality that the heartland of our faith is no longer the West. The centre of gravity has shifted South and East. Alister McGrath gives a telling example:

> On any given Sunday, there are now more Anglicans attending church in the West African state of Nigeria than in the United Kingdom, the United States, Canada and Australia, *taken together.* [6]

---

[6] Alister E. McGrath, *The Future of Christianity* (Malden, MA: Blackwell, 2002), p. x.

And here is a snapshot of the overall situation from a recent report prepared for Gordon Conwell Theological Seminary:

> The twentieth century experienced the great shift of Christianity to the global South, a trend that will continue into the future. In 1970, 41.3% of all Christians were from Africa, Asia, or Latin America. By 2020, this figure is expected to be 64.7%.[7]

How has this dramatic reorientation happened? In part, wonderfully, gloriously, through the explosive growth of the church in the South and East. In part, tragically, through the collapse of the church in the West. Yes, our western world has, historically, been deeply influenced by Christianity. But the age of Christendom in the West is past.

Loren Mead, in his insightful book, *The Once and Future Church*, outlines the key characteristics of the Christendom paradigm. Under Christendom the church exists as a parish within a Christian environment. Men and women are born into the faith, and, as Christians, function as good citizens of the Christian nation. The role of the churches in general, and the clergy in particular, is to act as chaplains to a Christian society. Christendom is a monolithic culture, meaning that all of society is gathered under the one Christian umbrella (much as Muslim countries gather under their one Islamic umbrella.) Thus under Christendom there is a unity of the sacred and secular.

---

[7] "Christianity in its Global Context, 1970-2020 Society, Religion, and Mission," Report Produced for the Center for the Study of Global Christianity, Gordon Conwell Theological Seminary (June 2013), p. 7.

Where is mission work done in a Christendom environment? It is carried out, by professional missionaries on the distant frontiers of the Christian world.[8]

We don't need much additional analysis to recognize this as a description of a world gone by, a remembered world, possibly a nostalgically remembered world, but not our present world. Pockets of Christendom may remain, but they only serve to make the point. Even to speak of "pockets of Christendom" is to announce the demise of that once monolithic culture.

And so we find ourselves today living in a situation much closer to the first centuries of Christianity. Mead describes some of the characteristics of that period. The church of those early days lived in a hostile environment. Christians did not identify with the surrounding culture. In fact the Greek word translated "church" comes from *ecclesia* meaning "called out ones." In the pre-Christendom age the boundaries of the church were very clear. You were either in or out. No one hung around the church if they were not serious about their allegiance to Jesus Christ. So the English word "witness" is translated from the Greek *marturos* which gives us (etymologically) our word "martyr." This was an environment where Christians regularly lost their lives for witnessing to their faith.

Where does mission work take place in this pre-Christian society? All church members are missionaries as soon as they step out into the streets of their own neighbourhoods.[9]

---

[8] Loren B. Mead, *The Once And Future Church: Reinventing The Congregation For A New Mission Frontier* (The Alban Institute, 1992 ed.), p. 13f.
[9] Ibid., p. 18.

This is the world of the book of Acts and the centuries immediately following. And today, at the beginning of the third millennium, we find ourselves living in an increasingly similar world.

But, of course, there is no true going back, history does not rewind. And though there are similarities with those early years there are also real differences. The memory and impact of Christendom lingers. It lingers in the corporate sub-consciousness of the West, shaped so deeply by the Christian faith. It lingers in the hearts of older generations who grew up with Christendom and who may, for a short while longer, dominate the leadership of the church. (Is this one of the reasons churches are slow to respond to the new reality?) It lingers also in places like the U.S. South where some sense of a Christian culture remains. Europe has traveled farthest down the road of post-Christendom. Canada lies somewhere between Europe and the U.S.

This post-Christendom era is in fact a period of ambiguity. The non-Christian world wavers between somewhat tolerant and somewhat hostile. But there is no question that the church that once played a dominant role in society is now at the margins. The church is no longer sure who she is and how she fits in. And as to what lies ahead we must wait and see. Alan Roxburgh describes the present detachment and loss of identity of the church using the term "liminality" (originally used to describe the no-man's land between childhood and adulthood in some folk cultures).[10]

---

[10] Alan J. Roxburgh, *The Missionary Congregation, Leadership, & Liminality* (Harrisburg, PA: Trinity Press International, 1997), p. 23f.

This liminal state is unnerving. Mead catches the mood: "An uncertain congregation then looks across an unfamiliar missionary frontier to an environment that appears less and less friendly and wonders." It wonders: about its identity; what the message is; how to deliver it; and what it means to be "called out."[11] The unrest affects the congregation itself. Once clear job descriptions are now blurred. Clergy and laity are forced to reinvent their roles. Clergy can no longer assume that authority comes with title, and there is little market for the chaplaincy work for which they were trained. The laity can no longer leave mission work to the professionals. Every member is a missionary as soon as she or he steps out of the door of the church.

This post-Christendom world is a place of ambiguity, unrest, and uncertainty. But surely, by God's grace, it is also a time of opportunity. For example, it is a time of increased clarity as the church stands out in bolder relief against a non-Christian background. Rodney Clapp writes of this costly but necessary, renewed clarity:

> So the grace is this: Christians feel useless because they are no longer useful for the wrong things, namely serving as chaplains in a sponsorial religion.[12]

Along with this we can expect to see an increase in committed Christians and a decrease in lukewarm Christians as we move forward into the 21st century.[13]

---

[11] Mead, p. 27.

[12] Rodney Clapp, *A Peculiar People: The Church As Culture In A Post-Christian Society* (Downers Grove, IL: InterVarsity Press, 1996), p. 23.

Churches that are willing to rediscover their missional identity are on the verge of a great adventure, not just because the old mission field has come to us (which is increasingly true in our mobile world) but because our own neighbourhoods are once again clearly recognizable as mission fields.

Some of the Epicurean and Stoic philosophers also conversed with him. And some said, "What does this babbler wish to say?" Others said, "He seems to be a preacher of foreign divinities"—because he was preaching Jesus and the resurrection. And they took him and brought him to the Areopagus, saying, "May we know what this new teaching is that you are presenting?

Acts 17:18-19

What a shake-up! Church leaders will need missionary training to be effective in this new environment. Indeed the whole congregation will seek missionary training. Yes, there will still be those knocking on the door of the church who were influenced by Christianity in their early years. But the pool of returning seekers is disappearing.[14] Christians will need to relearn the art of "initiating the conversation" with neighbours who have never had reason to take the Christian faith seriously, or as anything other than a historical anomaly. Paul's experience in Athens gives us the flavour of the challenge.

If, then, we accept that Christendom is past, how does this impact conversion?

---

[13] Lyle E. Schaller, *Discontinuity & Hope: Radical Change and the Path to the Future* (Nashville, TN: Abingdon, 1999), p. 226.

[14] Eddie Gibbs and Ian Coffey, *Church Next: Quantum Changes in Christian Ministry* (Leiscester, UK: InterVarsity, 2001), p. 171.

Firstly, it means that conversion involves a greater "distance of travel." This is a reference to the Engel Scale of Evangelism (developed by James Engel in the 1970s)[15] This is a way of charting the journey of faith. If someone begins with only a minimal awareness of the supernatural, let alone any knowledge of the God of Scripture, he or she will have to travel much further to get to the point of new birth than the person who is already familiar with the Christian Gospel and has already begun to be aware of the call to repentance and faith.

In our post-Christendom environment we can no longer assume that those we speak to will have even the most basic understanding of the Christian faith. In one baptism class I discovered that none of the people present knew how many Gospels there are in the New Testament. George Hunter saw this coming two decades ago: "We can now infer that, by the turn of the century, a third of all teenage and adult Americans will have no religious training in their background"[16]—make that two thirds for Canada. In this post-Christendom world new members will need more and deeper teaching.

Secondly, conversion is more costly. Under Christendom conversion was beneficial. In terms of society it was a coming onside, a joining. Leaders advertised their faith for political gain. Under post-Christendom, conversion is more like a betrayal, or at least aberrant, quirky behavior. "Can we trust these Jesus-followers?" society now asks. "Are they safe? . . . Will they put Canada first?"

---

[15] James F. Engel and Wilbert Norton, *What's Gone Wrong With the Harvest?: A Communication Strategy for the Church and World* (Zondervan, 1975).
[16] George G. Hunter III, *Church For The Unchurched* (Nashville, TN: Abingdon, 1996), p. 20.

Thirdly, conversion is less predictable. In earlier days, when the Christian faith was well known and understood far beyond the church walls, the transition into church-member status was a relatively smooth, well-worn path. Today potential church members are all over the map in terms of their understanding of the Christian faith, their expectations, their grasp of normative Christian behavior, and so on. The points of entry are increasingly diverse.

But fourthly, on the plus side, the problem of nominality (being Christians in name only) is greatly reduced. As our cultural environment shifts from tolerant to hostile, the new pilgrims give evidence of their sincerity simply by walking through the door of a church building. In the new world of the third millennium few people are interested in hanging around the church, or taking the name Christian, without a serious commitment to, and engagement with, the Lord Jesus Christ.

b) The Post-Modern World

We may be immersed in this post-modern world, but the concept of post-modernity is notoriously difficult to summarize in a few paragraphs. Let's begin by asking what is the post-modern world *post*? What was the *modern* world? and when?

Thomas Oden offers a couple of tidy book-ends for the phenomenon we label modernity—that period between 1789 (the storming of the Bastille) and 1989 (the collapse of the Berlin wall), i.e. from the French revolution to the collapse of communism. He sums up modernity as a mix of French Enlightenment, German Idealism, and British Empiricism.[17]

And to get a better grip on what all this means it is helpful to take a step even further back, to glance at the *pre-modern* world. Central to the world-view that preceded modernity was the idea of the supernatural. For the pre-modern mind the supernatural was an unquestioned part of reality. Human fulfillment, human life, required an understanding of, and a connection to, the supernatural. Reality extended beyond time into eternity.[18]

In sharp contrast to life under God, the age of modernity was about building a comprehensive understanding of the world, a metanarrative, built on a bedrock of rational certainty, with the supernatural banished from centre stage. Instead of the supernatural, human rational autonomy became the new lead actor. Religion did not disappear altogether, but it was delegated to the fringe, as a private concern only. Knowledge and progress, we were told, no longer needed to be anchored in the transcendent. Since history and tradition were irrecoverably tainted with the old superstitions (so it was thought) they too were dismissed to the sidelines. This was to be a fresh, clean start.

In the fulfilling of this grand project, complete objectivity, untainted by human prejudice, was both desirable and possible (so it was thought). As Mike Regele puts it: "Driven by the

---

[17] Thomas C. Oden, "The Death of Modernity and Postmodern Evangelical Spirituality" in *The Challenge of Postmodernism: An Evangelical Engagement* ed. David S. Dockery (Grand Rapids, MI: Baker, 2nd ed. 2001), p. 20f.
    [18] Millard J. Erickson, *Truth Or Consequences: The Promise & Perils of Postmodernism* (Downers Grove, IL: InterVarsity Press, 2001), p. 52.

goal of bombproof certainty, the pre-modern world was transformed into the modern world."[19] Thus human reason displaced divine authority, and individualism emerged as a primary characteristic of the period. Thomas Oden observes: "The key to modernity is the notion of choice—choosing oneself, and choosing for oneself over and against all traditional ways."[20]

This is the stripped-down, reductionist perspective that shaped, consciously or otherwise, the world view of our older generations today, including the older generations in our churches.

But modernity was a world that would not and could not last. In part, because the pristine objectivity required to guarantee "bombproof certainty" could not be secured. The reality is that we all see the world from our own particular angle. White, male Protestants simply do not read the data in the same way as Hispanic, female Catholics do, for example. It turns out that all truth is, to some extent, *interpreted.*

So the question was asked, Who is doing the interpreting? It became apparent that modernity's "objective truth" was remarkably allied with those holding greater power. Suspicion grew that truth claims were really power claims. (Thus the emergence of liberation movements of all kinds.)

Though tradition and religion could (temporarily at least) be dismissed, personal subjectivity could not. Modernity proved to be an unsustainable ideological construct. The goal

---

[19] Mike Regele, *Death of the Church* (Grand Rapids, MI: Zondervan, 1995), p. 63.
[20] Thomas C. Oden, *After Modernity . . . What?* (Grand Rapids, MI: Zondervan, 1990), pp. 74, 78.

of developing a Grand Narrative or Meta-Narrative, not only free from the so-called superstitions of the past, but also free of human subjectivity, had to be abandoned.

And as cracks were exposed in the "uni-verse" of modernity the "multi-verse" of post-modernity immerged. Instead of one truth, we have "your truth" and "my truth." Or, more often, "the truth of your tribe" and "the truth of my tribe." This "neo-tribalism" is being built, of course, not on common geography, but common narrative.

In a coffee shop in North Toronto, a friendly young man approached me and asked me what I was reading. When he discovered it was a Christian book he began earnestly to tell me about his own belief system. He was a member of the local Jedi Council (of the popular Star Wars movie series). Sensing my incredulity he explained further why this made sense for him.

But it was clear that we were not really communicating. A great gulf separated us, and the words we tossed back and forth drifted in meaning by the time they arrived on the other side. It struck me as a very post-modern conversation. We were members of parallel tribes living in parallel universes. Our narratives had coherence within our own tribe, but seemed incredible to the outside observer.

On the other hand there are limits to this post-modern fragmentation. My Jedi friend and I both paid for our coffee. We would both have ducked on coming to a low doorway. And possibly if we had continued talking we would have discovered we were common members of a third tribe—Chopin enthusiasts perhaps, or, less likely, the golfing community.

So the safest definition of post-modernity is simply that condition which followed modernity. It is not very helpful, but, by the nature of the situation, post-modernity cannot be bundled into a tidy package (tidy packages disappeared when modernity disappeared!) Post-modernity may be understood against the backdrop of modernity as in this sentence from Leonard Sweet:

> If the Modern Era was a rage for order, regulation, stability, singularity, and fixity, the Postmodern Era is a rage for chaos, uncertainty, otherness, openness, multiplicity, and change.[21]

To this we can add another curious characteristic of post-modernity. The implosion of modernity has freed post-moderns to take seriously, once again, the wisdom and achievements of earlier ages. In the age of post-modernity the pre-modern world is back on the radar.

This is not the place to pursue the notion of post-modernity in depth but we must acknowledge the pervasive influence of this new philosophical climate if we want to understand our times. No corner of current culture is untouched.

A public and readily visible instance of this is post-modern architecture. Where the architecture of modernity (following the philosophy of modernity) was all about efficiency, stripped of all allusion to unnecessary historical precedent (think of the plain, glass and concrete structures of the 70s and 80s), post-modern architecture once again incorporates classical architectural themes, though often in whimsical and humourous ways (think of castle roofs and gargoyles on contemporary residential high-rises).

---

[21] Leonard Sweet, *AquaChurch* (Loveland, CO: Group, 1999), p. 24.

A good example of post-modern architecture is Library Square (built 1995) in downtown Vancouver. At the heart of the structure is the sleek, glass, nine-story block, housing book stacks and offices. This is surrounded by a massive, ornate, elliptical exterior, clearly modeled on the well-known Roman Coliseum of classical times. The complex includes a vast, covered, cathedral-like, multipurpose, public space. The chief architect was the famous Israeli-Canadian, Moshe Safdie. Such a curious mingling of ancient and contemporary design would never have seen the light of day in the climate of modernity.

And no corner of the church is untouched by post-modernity. This is evident in such characteristics as the skepticism towards authority, the loss of allegiance to organizational structure, and the increased appreciation for sacred space, mystery, and tradition. This new cultural climate has opened the door to a new appreciation of classical Christianity as it was, in the words of Robert Webber, "shaped by mystery, holism, interpreted facts, community, and a combination of verbal and symbolic forms of communication." He goes so far as to suggest that "no Christian dare wrestle with post-modern thought until she or he has studied classical Christian thought."[22] What a change from 50 years ago. Our society's shift from modernity to post-modernity has challenged Christians to disentangle from modernity also. We'll come back to this later.

---

[22] Robert Webber, *Ancient-Future Faith: Rethinking Evangelicalism for a Postmodern World* (Grand Rapids, MI: Baker, 1999), pp. 24, 29.

Has modernity disappeared altogether in the church?—no. Just as many church members still sport their faded Christendom hats, post-moderns, moderns, and pre-moderns now often share the same pew. Pre-moderns also?—yes. Think of immigrants from traditional, non-western cultures, for example. Our formative early years greatly shape the way we experience the remainder of our lives, even if rather incongruently in radically different environments.

Furthermore as Os Guinness points out, though modernism, as a way of *thinking*, has collapsed, the *techniques* of modernity are "stronger than ever."[23] This can be a good thing. Who would want to go back to pre-modern days in the field of dentistry, for example! But the techniques of modernity are not value-neutral. Guinness is particularly concerned that proponents of the so-called "church growth movement" have used tools of modernity, "from the fields of management, marketing, psychology, and communications," uncritically, and are impoverished accordingly.[24]

If modernity was a mixed blessing, the question now is just how far should Christians distance themselves from that worldview. Albert Mohler[25] is concerned that Christians, rebounding from toxic modernity, will swallow too much of toxic post-modernity and end up as cynics. Or, to use the philosophical jargon, they will "assume incredulity towards the

---

[23] Os Guinness, *Dining With The Devil: The Megachurch Movement Flirts With Modernity* (Grand Rapids, MI: Baker, 1993), p. 19.
[24] Ibid., p. 13.
[25] R. Albert Mohler, "The Integrity of the Evangelical Tradition and the Challenge of the Postmodern Paradigm" in Dockery, p. 53f.

Christian metanarrative" in an ill-advised, over-reaching attempt to engage with the present age.

But we don't need to go that far. Regele argues for a middle ground (as does Erickson). There is good reason to be content with "relative certainty," without taking up the (lost) cause of "absolute certainty" on the one hand, or the (despairing) cause of "radical relativism" on the other.[26]

Does this post-modern middle ground mean that we must abandon the very concept of absolute truth? Certainly not. We Christians acknowledge that God knows all things, and knows them truly. And one day we, too, will know as he knows. As Paul writes, looking ahead to the day when he stands in the presence of his Lord:

> For now we see in a mirror dimly, but then face to face. Now I know in part; *then I shall know fully*, even as I have been fully known (1 Corinthians 13:12, italics mine).

But for now, on this side of eternity, we are wise to retain the same humility that Paul had. For various reasons we, too, see only "dimly." Primarily, because sin has affected and infected our ability to evaluate truth. Too often we evaluate truth selfishly and arrogantly. Too often our thumb is on the scales. By God's grace, and by his Spirit, we are getting cleansed of our sin. But we do not expect to be fully sanctified in this life. Thus our truth assessments retain their margin of error.

What, then, does this mean for our proclamation of the Christian faith in our world? Has all confidence been stripped

---

[26] Regele, p. 77f.

away? Again we say, certainly not. We are relatively certain of many things, and we could say "adequately certain" of much. Are we not certain enough of our core beliefs that we are ready to die for them?

And are we not at least as certain as other tribes are of *their* belief systems? We have every right to bring our story to the table, and also to challenge, respectfully, other stories. "How is your belief system working for you?" we might ask. "Does it really cohere as well as you think? What about this? or that? Let me tell you how Jesus makes sense of my world."

But the tone of our voice, as we communicate this Gospel we are willing to die for, will need to be softened. Post-modern evangelists need a kinder, gentler approach than has often been used in the past. Chuck Smith writes, "In modernity, Christians learned how to monologue eloquently. Now we must learn how to dialogue."[27] In this post-modern world with its deep suspicion of authority and metanarrative, evangelists need a new humility, and a willingness to come alongside and share the journey.

Furthermore, in this new, post-rational environment, the old standby of apologetics has a reduced role in bringing people to the point of conversion. Apologetics is now more useful for believers than unbelievers. In the church, as in society, relationship has taken priority over reason. So we notice that people now often belong before they believe.

In its more extreme forms post-modernity fractures our ability to communicate. There is little common language that

---

[27] Chuck Smith, *The End of the World As We Know It: Clear Directions For Bold and Innovative Ministry In a Postmodern World* (Colorado Springs, CO: WaterBrook, 2001), p. 196.

allows one tribe to dialogue with another.[28] Words that sound the same are defined differently by different tribes. We get nowhere by simply turning up the volume. Post-modern guru Richard Rorty suggests that his own philosophy should not be presented and argued for, piece by piece, but allowed to stand as a whole—to be accepted or rejected as a block.[29]

We see an interesting parallel in the church, as we welcome people to come alongside our Christian word and life, encouraging the new pilgrims to mingle with our tribe, until a paradigm shift occurs and they embrace the Christian world view holistically. The post-modern heart is not won through fighting inch by inch, but by being present with integrity, and authenticity, and love. We remember that line from Blaise Pascal: "The heart has its reasons that reason knows not of."

> *Trust in the LORD with all your heart, and do not lean on your own understanding.*
>
> Proverbs 3:5

We can note in passing the increased profile of *shame* in this new environment. Guilt is about what I did; shame is about who I am. Guilt is about breach of rules; shame is about breach of relationships, about being seen negatively by others. In the brave, individualistic world of modernity we cared little what others thought. Now the haunting question of post-moderns is, "Will my tribe accept me?" For the new pilgrims, sin's *shame* burden may weigh more than sin's *guilt* burden. Redemption from shame brings a new urgency to Christian conversion in the age of post-modernity.

---

[28] Gary Phillips, "Religious Pluralism in a Postmodern World" in Dockery, p. 131f.
[29] Erickson, p. 159.

How good it is to remember then, that Jesus, immersed as he was in an honour-shame culture, delivered people from both guilt *and* shame. And today we are recovering more of the wholeness of his ministry as we rediscover Gospel resources for shame as well as guilt. (For a book-length treatment of this subject see my *Grace for Shame*.[30])

Conversion in people shaped by post-modernity may appear less defined, less dependent on abstract reason, more ambiguous, more relational, more process oriented. Post-moderns are more comfortable with paradox and mystery than their immediate predecessors. They may be touched by sacred space and form, though not by the institutions that sponsor these. The new pilgrims do have a spiritual hunger, but they will not fit the tidy categories of old modernity's Christianity.

So the condition of post-modernity brings its own questions to the subject of conversion. For example (to use a well worn question) if I die tonight, am I "absolutely certain" I will go to heaven? or am I "relatively certain"? or is there no way of knowing? Does mere "relative certainty" constitute substandard faith? Is it even possible for post-moderns to be saved?

Yet, as so many will readily testify, the post-modern middle ground of *adequate* certainty is able to satisfy our heart hunger. There is a relational knowing that grips us more deeply than a rational knowing alone. In the words of Romans 8:16, "The Spirit himself bears witness with our spirit that we are children of God," and we find ourselves at peace.

---

[30] John A. Forrester, *Grace for Shame: The Forgotten Gospel* (Pastor's Attic Press, 2014).

c) The Post-Boomer World

Through the 80's and 90's, especially in the U.S., many of the mega churches (and much of the church growth movement) rode the "Boomer wave." Middle-aged Baby Boomers felt compelled to deal with what Wade Clark Roof calls the inner "empty waste."[31] They set out on a spiritual quest and the church, in part at least, rose to the occasion. So that Chuck Smith can write

> What shocked me most about my twenty-year class reunion was the number of people in my graduating class who had become devout Christians—they all seemed so pagan in high school.[32]

But the crest of that wave has passed. By now most of that generation is long-past the so-called "mid-life passage," that time, for so many, of one last search for the deeper meaning of life. By now, most of the Boomers are settling in for a comfortable retirement.[33] They have their ducks all nicely in a row.

And while it is admittedly premature to suggest this is a post-Boomer world—aging Boomers will still have a huge influence over the next few decades—it is true that churches must be increasingly attuned to the vastly different characteristics of the succeeding generations if they are to thrive and grow. As Lyle Schaller argues, "For most congregations, the central 'either-or' issue is adapt to a new era

---

[31] Wade Clark Roof, *Spiritual Marketplace: Baby Boomers and the Remaking of American Religion* (Princeton, NJ: Princeton UP, 1999), p. 16.
[32] Chuck Smith, p. 167.
[33] Roof, p. 59.

or watch your members grow older in age and fewer in number."[34]

A familiarity with generation theory is just one more example of how pastors are now called on to venture beyond their traditional categories of learning. The living generations are commonly delineated as: *Builders* (born 1901-1924), *Silents* (born 1925-1942), *Boomers* (born 1943-1960), *GenXers* (born 1961-1981), *Millennials* (born 1982-early 2000s),[35] and the yet to be named, currently still-in-formation generation.

Each generation has its own characteristics. Which is why evangelistic welcome mats put out for Boomers (think rock and roll worship, warehouse meeting-places, super-sized congregations, and the "seeker-sensitive" consumer orientation) may have little impact on GenXers and Millennials. And matters are further complicated by the realization that generations in the U.S. may have different characteristics from same generations in other countries (differences often ignored in the influential U.S. literature.[36])

The general pattern has been for dominant generations to alternate with recessive generations. Yet while the U.S. Boomers are dominant, Canadian (plus U.K. and European) Boomers are recessive. John Zimmerman argues that it is in fact the U.S. generations that are out of sync. The U.S. skipped a generation due to the trauma of its Civil War. As a result U.S. generations are one step ahead in the cycle.[37]

---

[34] Lyle E. Schaller, *The New Reformation: Tomorrow Arrived Yesterday* (Nashville, TN: Abingdon, 1995), p. 53.

[35] Regele, p. 114.

[36] For example, Regele often, and Richard Kew, *Brave New Church: What The Future Holds* (Harrisburg, PA: Morehouse, 2001), p. 19.

[37] John C. Zimmerman, "Leadership Across the Gaps Between Generations," *Crux* 31, no. 2 (June 1995): p. 49f.

Zimmerman's article provides needed insight into the differences between Canada and the U.S. But his work could be developed further, especially in regard to later generations. GenXers and Millennials are the first *global* generations. Thus we can expect these younger cohorts to be drawn into alignment regardless of geographic location. Furthermore, given the pervasive and persuasive nature of U.S. culture, same-age generations in other countries will tend to edge in that direction.

But it is helpful, particularly in regard to the Boomer generation, to acknowledge these differences. For example, Boomer oriented church plants in Canada that followed U.S. formats generally fizzled. Gibbs notes that "British Boomers have more in common with urban GenXers and Millennials in the USA in terms of social attitudes."[38] While Canadian GenXers are more in touch with global issues than U.S. GenXers and have a greater environmental consciousness.

Keeping in mind these nuances what can we learn about what has been called (in U.S. terms) the "Thirteenth Generation"[39]—Generation X? We begin by acknowledging that this generation began as Christendom ended. This means that most of the assumptions we made about people who had grown up in a Christian environment don't apply to Generation X and succeeding generations. Conversion begins "much further back" as noted earlier. We cannot assume even a basic understanding of the Christian faith.

---

[38] Gibbs, 2001, p. 222f.
[39] Tom Beaudoin, *Virtual Faith: The Irreverent Spiritual Quest of Generation X* (San Francisco, CA: Jossey-Bass, 1998), p. 27.

This doesn't mean that GenXers are religionless, far from it. But their spirituality draws from Hinduism, Buddhism, Muslim and pagan religions as much as from Christianity.[40] Furthermore, there is a strong *experience* orientation in GenX spirituality. "There is a constant yearning, both implicit and explicit, for the almost mystical encounter of the human and the divine."[41] It will seem odd to older generations that the suffering of Christ strikes a chord with GenXers, who have found life much more difficult than the materially prosperous Boomers. Hence the prevalence of the cross as an accessory (or tattoo).

Oh that you would rend the heavens and come down, that the mountains might quake at your presence.

Isaiah 64:1

Smith argues that the conversion of Generation X will begin with a conversion of the church. He sketches the changes: "[GenX] churches will be dynamic rather than static, experiential rather than cerebral, and more like a party than a funeral."[42] It will also begin with a pastoral conversion. Those who minister to GenXers will need to recognize that institutional authority carries no weight for younger generations. They will need a new humility. They will be responsive to GenXers' hunger for older, classical forms of spirituality (not to mention their more eclectic musical appetite—hymnic fusions of Celtic, classical, jazz, ethnic, and contemporary.) They will learn to be comfortable with a more flexible, inclusive, ambiguous, communal, spiritual world.

---

[40] Ibid., p. 25.
[41] Ibid., p. 74.
[42] Chuck Smith, p. 165.

Conversion looks different for the new pilgrims of this post-Boomer environment. It is less individualistic and more relational. It is less head and more heart. It is less consumer-oriented and more participatory. These younger converts are sending us back to the Bible with fresh questions.

And surely this is good news. As a consequence we are relearning the length and breadth, the height and depth, of God's saving grace. The Gospel of God is for Gen-Xers and Millennials too!

d) The Post-Monocultural World

Of course, we never really did live in a monocultural world. Canada is a country of immigrants. Vancouver, on the edge of the Pacific, was, from early days, home to Japanese fishermen, and Chinese shop keepers and railroad workers, as well as Scottish bankers, English bricklayers and Italian tile setters.

But globalization has brought an exponential increase in travel and immigration. The rising economies of the East mean recent Asian immigrants now settle in the wealthiest neighbourhoods (rather than "across the tracks"). The new Chinatown is an upscale mall. It was possible to hide from diversity in the past; now, at the beginning of the third millennium, it is unavoidable. According to Statistics Canada, in Vancouver proper only 50% claim English as their mother tongue. In some schools 70% of students are learning English as a second language and the lack of English students is making it difficult for these newcomers to make progress.

Globalization means the mixing of cultures and the increase in multicultural schools, communities and churches.

Epidemics and economics may, from time to time, interrupt this trend, but globalization is here to stay. In fact, physical relocation is only one aspect of globalization. As mentioned earlier there is a global interconnectedness among the younger generation that is nurtured by the interconnected digital world. Even as older folk are struggling to come to terms with the new mix of race and culture, it is already a non-issue for most younger people who have adjusted and moved on.

What impact does this cultural mixing have on the church? A negative concern is the homogenization of spirituality. An increasingly generic culture can yield an increasingly generic Christianity.[43] So we have sung the same Christian songs in London, Nanjing, Manila, Istanbul, and Vancouver—how boring!

On the other hand this conjunction of cultures may also act as a corrective. Sharon Kim shows how first and second generation Korean immigrants, traditionally having strong authoritarian, top-down power structures, have moved to more participatory and egalitarian decision-making patterns as they have interacted with other cultures.[44]

We learn a lot from other ways and other perspectives. Just as GenXers and Millennnials alert us to forgotten fields of grace, so do other races and cultures as they bring their own strengths and questions to the word and work of God. This diversity we must preserve. As Erickson observes:

---

[43] Roof, p. 72f.
[44] Sharon Kim, "Creating Campus Communities: Second-Generation Korean-American Ministries at UCLA" in *GenX Religion,* eds. Richard W. Flory and Donald E. Miller (New York, NY: Routledge, 2000), p. 103.

Multiculturalism is important, not because all cultures are equally acceptable and true for their own group but because no one culture has the entire truth.[45]

Life in the global village produces a tension between the desire for pluralism and multicultural acceptance, and the pull to tribalism and the urge to preserve identity. The genius of the church is that, at best, it is a place where distinctive cultures are preserved and respected, while still finding unity in Christ. Even when we barely share a common language, the sense of belonging to one family is remarkable. So the increasing cultural diversity of both major cities, like Vancouver and Toronto, and hundreds of lesser towns between, has encouraged the emergence of numerous multicultural congregations.

And people will come from east and west, and from north and south, and recline at table in the kingdom of God.

Luke 13:29

Suddenly those of us who "want to be a New Testament church" have remembered that New Testament churches were international! Think of the leadership team of the church in Antioch (Acts 13:1): Barnabas (a Jewish Cypriot believer), Simeon "called Niger" (dark-complexioned), Lucius "of Cyrene" (Libya, north Africa), Manaen (brought up with Herod the tetrarch in Palestine), and Saul (a Jew from Tarsus)—five diverse leaders from three continents. And by Acts 16 and the start of the Macedonian churches we see both cultural *and* gender diversity. Schaller comments that the greater role of

---

[45] Erickson, p. 194.

women, and the decline in racial barriers, are two of the markers of the "New Reformation."[46]

What impact does our multicultural environment have on conversion? Firstly, it affects our communication of the Gospel. Loewen rightly emphasizes the need for "an attitude of reciprocity" which includes "an honest acceptance of each others' cultures," "a spirit of exchange," and "personal and cultural self-exposure."[47] In short, pastors need the open heart and mind of a missionary. We will be patient as we search for words that cross not only language gaps, but cultural gaps.

Secondly, we must not expect "cookie-cutter" conversions. In culturally diverse contexts and congregations we need to be alert to the reality that conversion will look and feel different for different cultures. For example, some people will simply not respond to the traditional call to "come forward" (as a sign of responding to the Christian Gospel).

Donald Jacobs describes some of the complexities. We need to recognize that Christian conversion will be shaped by cultural expectations (we may become more aware of how our own conversions have been shaped by western expectations.) For some cultures it will be very important that Jesus Christ replaces the former "primary source of power." Thus one culture should resist defining "normative" for another culture. Each must determine its own "symbols of conversion." At the same time each culture must bow before Scripture.[48]

---

[46] Schaller 1995, p. 27.

[47] Jacob Loewen, "The Gospel: Its Content and Communication—An Anthropological Perspective," in Coote, p. 127f.

[48] Donald R. Jacobs, "Conversion and Culture—An Anthropological Perspective with Reference to East Africa," in Coote, p. 144f.

To this list we can add that most immigrants are coming from cultures that are far more shame-oriented than our guilt-oriented western cultures. We know how to minister grace for guilt, do we know how to minister grace for shame?

Closely related to this is the way the reduced emphasis on individualism in some cultures is reshaping the face of conversion in our churches. Our group-oriented Asian friends often convert to the community, then convert to the Lord of the community (which is now also evident in younger home-grown seekers). Community-oriented peoples need a new community to call home if they are to leave the old community. Standing alone is not a realistic option for them. They need to be reborn into a *family*. So in a multicultural environment it is especially important that evangelism be understood as the work of the church as a *community* rather than the work of one or two gifted individuals.

Pastors are now called to nurture evangelistic communities that are willing to embrace the newcomer and the culture of the newcomer. Thus, as Clapp points out,[49] one problem with Richard Niebuhr's classic *Christ and Culture* is that Christ is set over against culture (singular). While in reality the world is a mosaic of cultures that we constantly intersect, and the church is one of these alternate cultures.

In fact the church itself must undergo a kind of cultural conversion as the congregation becomes increasingly diverse. The host culture must also be willing to "leave home" (as in a marriage[50]) so that there will be an equal partnership—not *them* becoming like *us*, but together establishing a new home.

---

[49] Clapp, p. 174.
[50] Genesis 2:24

We do well to remember, after all, that Jesus was not a white guy. We of European background may turn out to be more distant from the Middle-Eastern cultures of the Bible than many of the so-called foreigners knocking on the doors of our church buildings. Perhaps our Lord has sent these new pilgrims to us so that we may see him more clearly.

e) The Post-Liberal World

One of the ironies of the late 20th century was the uncomfortable discovery that both theological liberals and theological fundamentalists had each, in their own way, hitched their wagons to the rising star of modernity. It was uncomfortable because the star of modernity unfortunately morphed into a plummeting meteor. Hence, the post-liberal world.

Once again, to say post-liberal is perhaps to overstate the case. But the tide has long since turned. Alister McGrath sees 1977 as the "high water mark of classical theological liberalism" in the U.K. Since then conservative Christianity has surged forward.[51] He notes, for example, on the Canadian scene, the emergence of Regent College in Vancouver and Tyndale College and Seminary in Toronto, both evangelical institutions, as the largest theological schools in the country.[52] And he predicts that the next 100 years of Christianity will be shaped by four movements: Roman Catholicism, Pentecostal-

---

[51] Quoted by Kew, p. 129.
[52] McGrath, p. 112.

ism, evangelicalism, and Eastern Orthodoxy. Mainline Protestantism is the obvious omission.[53]

Philip Jenkins describes the explosive growth of Christianity in the Southern hemisphere. He argues that not only is the centre of gravity now in the south, that centre has also shifted from liberal to conservative, as southern churches of all stripes focus on their Scriptural roots.[54]

What was the connection between liberal theology and modernity? The term liberal theology embraces a wide range of positions but at heart it rose as a response to the threat of modernity. The modern world wanted to begin with a clean slate, to brush aside the prejudices of tradition and inherited belief systems, and make a fresh beginning using only the distilled water of reason. Christians, who had, for so long, played a central and privileged role in the development of the West, now found their religion a liability rather than an asset. Modernity had no patience for ancient creeds, or church authority, or distant texts, or (especially) the supernatural.

As Christians scrambled to retain a place of dignity in this new and frosty environment many consciously or otherwise bought into modernity's

The same day Sadducees came to him, who say that there is no resurrection, and they asked him a question . . .

But Jesus answered them, "You are wrong, because you know neither the Scriptures nor the power of God."

Matthew 22:23, 29

---

[53] Ibid., p. 99.

[54] Philip Jenkins, "The Next Christianity," *Atlantic Monthly*, October 2002.

agenda of giving human reason primacy of place. The notion of the authority of divine revelation was quietly slipped to the back burner.

This had a profound impact on theology. The ethical claims of Christianity could be sustained (for the time being) but supernatural claims were all suspect. How could a modern rational mind accept the doctrines of the virgin birth? the resurrection? or the physical return of Jesus? So the teachings of Christian orthodoxy came under the scrutiny and judgment of secular human reason.

We can feel the defensive theological climate behind a book title such as *Religion: Speeches to its Cultured Despisers* (1799) by Friedrich Schleiermacher (who dodged the claims of reason by arguing that religion was primarily about feelings and intuition), and 150 years later in Rudolf Bultmann's "Demythologizing" agenda (he, too, was attempting to make an ancient belief palatable to modern technologically advanced men and women).

But this liberal approach could not stand, for at least two reasons. Firstly, once the supernatural aspects of Christianity were pared away, the ethical and moral claims could not be sustained either—we cannot be good without God. Foundational to the New Testament story is the promise of the gift of the Holy Spirit, who takes up residence in the followers of Jesus to sanctify us and to bear the fruit of a godly character.

Secondly, there was a limited market for a religion stripped down to a minimalist God. Spiritually hungry people are looking for a robust encounter with the Divine. Christianity has been a powerful force precisely because it is otherworldly.

People instinctively comprehend that we need to look for help *Beyond Ourselves* (to borrow a book title from the conservative camp).

Furthermore, with the collapse of modernity (at least as philosophical stance), liberal theology has lost its *reason d'etre*. Myth, Mystery, and the Supernatural, are back in!

The future is not entirely bleak for theologically liberal churches. But where liberalism survives with any strength today it does so by moving closer to orthodoxy. Paradoxically the style and form of many theologically liberal churches are often more conservative than their theologically conservative counterparts. Younger generations have a renewed appreciation for traditional buildings, and may find the look, feel, smell and sound of tradition more appealing. Post-moderns may also find the often less strident (more humble?) tone of the wiser liberal churches more palatable.

But will these new pilgrims find conversion? By the grace of God they may. Nevertheless, authentic conversion rests on the very areas liberal theology has been uncomfortable with: the supernatural intervention of God; the historicity of the salvation event; and the transforming power of an authoritative, Spirit-inspired text.

f) The Post-Fundamentalist World

Fundamentalism immerged in reaction to liberal theology and the secularization of the church. The irony, as we have noted, is that both liberalism and fundamentalism felt obliged to make sense of the world using the principles and priorities of modernity. Oden states this thought succinctly:

> Fundamentalism could not have happened in any century prior to the nineteenth . . . Modern fundamentalism is more akin to liberalism than either one of them would be willing to admit. Both tacitly assumed that faith was based on objective historical evidence and both were over-confident of their forms of evidence.[55]

Roof adds his voice noting that both the "dogmatists" (fundamentalists) and the "secularists" (liberals) are the "fallout from the raging storm known as modernity."[56]

To use Regele's terminology, fundamentalists bought into the modernist agenda of developing an "unassailable foundation of truth."[57] But such taking up of the world's weapons proved to be a great hindrance to the church. Fundamentalism, caught up as it was in modernity's reductionist agenda, focused too much on historical proofs and neglected issues of broader significance. Fundamentalism was too much a child of modernity to be truly orthodox.[58] With the vine of modernity all but dead, fundamentalism's days are numbered. And with the waning of liberalism its own *reason d'etre* is gone also.

Gibbs comments: "[Evangelicalism] was itself influenced, more than it realized, by the modernism it combated."[59] Stanley Grenz takes this a step further by arguing that in some ways evangelicalism itself "with its focus on scientific thinking, the

---

[55] Oden, p. 67f.
[56] Roof, p. 214.
[57] Regele, p. 63.
[58] Oden, p. 66f.
[59] Gibbs 2001, p. 27.

empirical approach, and common sense—is a child of early modernity."[60] While Grenz may over-estimate the parallels between fundamentalism and evangelicalism and under estimate the ability of evangelicalism to take in a wider embrace of philosophical positions, there are concerns for one aspect of this movement—evangelical revivalism.

The roots of revivalism go back to John Wesley at least. But the modern shape of revivalism (at least in its highly influential American form) stems from the ministry of Charles Finney (1792-1875). In its modern manifestation we see that revivalism is closely linked to the rise of fundamentalism in practice and in spirit. Which is why many observers of Christianity somewhat loosely equate fundamentalism with revivalism.

Revivalism reveals its links with modernity in, for example, its love of technique. Technique gets results. Revival is practically guaranteed if the prescription of prayer and repentance is followed. But is God "on call" really God? Is this not putting human beings in the driver's seat? This brings us close to the human-centred spirit of modernity.

Notice how technique is applied to conversion itself. Smith points out the modern worldview behind "The Four Spiritual Laws" (a commonly used evangelistic formula)—it reflects a mechanical (modern) view of the universe.[61] While it may be helpful to present the salvation story in simple point form we need to keep in mind what is lost and what is added. What is lost is the biblical richness of narrative and metaphor.

---

[60] Stanley J. Grenz, "Star Trek and the Next Generation: Postmodernism and the Future of Evangelical Theology," in Dockery, p. 82.
[61] Chuck Smith, p. 92f.

Was not Jesus a consummate story-teller and a weaver of unforgettable parables? What is added is an air of precipitous urgency that reflects a modern's view of clock time and the drive for efficiency.

The influence of modernity is also apparent in the emphasis on getting people to a "decision." And so we sometimes see Revivalism further reduced to Decisionism. Converts do need to make a decision, but volition is only one element of conversion, as we will see. Decisionism betrays an inadequate view of conversion because: (a) it over-focuses on boundary crossing to the neglect of ongoing transformation; (b) it ignores the complexity of conversion, and; (c) it over-emphasizes the human component of conversion. Decisionism, with its need-to-know-for-sure, time-and-place addiction, is an offspring of modernity. As such it may do more harm than good. As we will see later, if the foundations of conversion are not well and thoroughly laid, it is difficult to move on. Guinness frames the concern starkly: "Modernity simultaneously makes evangelism infinitely easier but discipleship infinitely harder."[62]

Revivalism was also the attempt to bring back to life what was assumed to be present—a latent Christian faith. As such it

> *Besides this*
> *you know the time . . .*
> *For salvation*
> *is nearer to us now*
> *than when we first believed.*
> *The night is far gone;*
> *the day is at hand.*
> *So then let us cast off*
> *the works of darkness and*
> *put on the armor of light.*
>
> Romans 13:11, 12

---

[62] Guinness, p. 43.

was inherently a feature of a Christendom paradigm.[63] We are now in a post-revivalism situation simply by being in a post-Christendom situation. (We cannot revive what has never lived!) Thus with the loss of Christendom it is important to distinguish revivalism from evangelism. Evangelism continues. Evangelism brings Good News to those who never knew as well as to those who once knew. Revivalism brought closure: evangelism creates openings.

As the deep freeze of modernity recedes, the drifting ice flows of liberalism and fundamentalism are both melting fast. Nothing is to be gained from jumping back and forth. What is needed is a leap to *terra firma*—a Christianity more broadly grounded in Scripture, a Christianity that does not forget the past but learns from both the highs and lows of 2000 years of doing church, and then moves on. Leonard Sweet puts this well:

> To live faithfully in the twenty-first century, we must live out of the full two-thousand-year history of the Christian church and not lobotomize the last nineteen centuries to get back to the first century. God did not put us through the past two thousand years for no good reason.[64]

How has our understanding of conversion deepened as we exit the age of modernity which indirectly fostered and sustained fundamentalism and its cousin, revivalist evangelicalism? This new climate thrusts upon us new questions and new perspectives. Post-modernity teaches us to

---

[63] Clapp, p. 153.
[64] Sweet, p. 72.

be more comfortable with the *ambiguity* that often accompanies the Christian pilgrimage. We are learning to accept conversion as a *process* as well as an event. Indeed, has it not always been so? Hunter gives an example:

> Studies of autobiographical accounts of eighteenth-century Methodists indicate that the gap in time between people's awakening and their experience of justification *averaged* about two years.[65]

Furthermore revivalism neglected the *ecclesiology* of conversion. But our post-modern world has reminded us of the necessity of relationships and the dangers of individualism. We discover that it may not be best (or even true) that "one wins another" to Christ, but that most people come to Christ as they encounter a living community of faith. In another blow to the idolatry of the individual we may even find (horrors!) a *corporate* coming to faith—group conversions—and discover, furthermore, that this too is biblical (a *household* converted, Acts 16:31f., or even a *whole city* converted, Jonah 3:7-10).

Fundamentalism was an important arm of the church through modernity. We honour those heroes who held to the fundamentals of the faith in contrary times. And so we may mourn the passing of fundamentalism. But we have not lost the faith. We still must, and will be, by God's grace, "born again." And perhaps the new pilgrims of this present age have the opportunity to be born again even more profoundly now, than under the reductionist agenda of modernity.

---

[65] Hunter, p. 154.

Summary

If we Christians wonder why our world feels different, these
are some of the causes. The church in the West is speaking to a
new audience. We cannot assume this audience has any
understanding of who we are.
They may find us an irritant or
simply irrelevant. Furthermore it
is an incredibly diverse audience.
Thus our message will need to be
less confrontational and more
conciliatory than it has often
been, more humble, more
dialogue less monologue, more heart less head. Our message
will need to be lived out in community—warm, welcoming,
hospitable.

. . . of [the tribe of] Issachar,
men who had
understanding of the times,
to know what Israel
ought to do.
1 Chronicles 12:32

We must be willing to allow the new prilgrims to make
the long journey to faith, being patient, walking alongside,
respecting diversity, listening much, yet still ready to share our
unique story. We will be surprised by the renewed influence of
the deep past, of sacred space and symbol, of mystery and
sacrament. We will find little patience for institutions and
authorities. But we will also find a thirst for authenticity and a
hunger for God.

One more note. Where there is change there is always
loss. And where there is loss there is always grief and all that
accompanies grief—shock, denial, bargaining, anger, blame,
despair, and so on, before reaching the place of acceptance and
hope.

And we see all these responses at the beginning of this
new millennium. Champions of Christendom circle the wagons

and fight for 1950. Defenders of "cultural purity" call angrily for changes to immigration laws. Children of modernity despair of the "woolly-headed" post-moderns. Pillars of the church lament the "lack of commitment" of younger generations. Liberal brothers and sisters accuse the evangelicals of turning fundamentalist. Fundamentalist brothers and sisters accuse the evangelicals of turning liberal. Suddenly there are new ways to suffer in pastoral ministry!

But this is also a day of great opportunity. People have a new curiosity about this odd tribe who claim to follow Jesus. Against the backdrop of our neo-pagan neighbourhoods the ancient Christian faith jumps out in greater relief. True, conversion is less predictable in this complex new world—less manageable—at least for us (who love to manage!) But it is God who converts and who will continue to convert. Nothing of this new day is a surprise to him. And the glorious call to join his cause is surely no less compelling now than it was in that once familiar world fast disappearing in the rear-view mirror.

2. New Thinking About Conversion

We turn now to four writers who demonstrate the way in which this new and uneasy environment is bringing new questions to bear on the subject of conversion.

a) Richard Peace, *Conversion in the New Testament: Paul and the Twelve* (Grand Rapids, MI: Eerdmans, 1999)

Richard Peace began his evangelistic ministry with an understanding of conversion that regarded Paul's Damascus road experience as the model:

> Conversion . . . involved saying yes to Jesus by means of a simple prayer of repentance and faith . . . it was sudden, singular, emotional, and instantaneously transforming (2).[66]

But then Peace began to encounter people who appeared to be orthodox believers, committed to Christ, but who "could not define the moment when they arrived at such a commitment" (2). While others appeared to have a genuine

---

[66] Beginning here the numbers in parenthesis are the page numbers in Peace.

conversion experience yet their life and attitude to others showed little change.

This challenge to his assumptions about conversion drove Peace back to the New Testament for further study and reflection and eventually led him to focus on Mark's Gospel. Peace became convinced that what Mark was describing in his Gospel was "the unfolding conversion of the Twelve" (4). Mark was describing conversion as a *journey* not an *event*.

Peace lays out his material in three movements. First he establishes a foundation by examining the conversion of Paul. Second he presents his analysis of Mark's Gospel. Third he suggests some adjustments (to methods of evangelism) that take into account this "unfolding process" where conversion takes place over time. What follows is a brief review of each section.

First, then, Paul's conversion. It is common to refer to Paul's conversion as normative. Peace examines Paul's conversion to define the "core pattern." He observes three elements: insight, turning, and transformation. Each stage is essential for full conversion, he tells us.

> At the core of the concept of conversion is the idea of turning. On the one side of that turning are the conditions that facilitate or enable the turning to take place (insight). On the other side of the turning is the outcome or result of the turning (transformation) (37).

Peace then brings this pattern to Mark's Gospel. Here the situation is different. These men are not notorious sinners (as Paul was). Their change takes place over an extended period of time (not in a flash). They are changed—but is this conversion?

Peace says yes. The disciples do experience a New Testament conversion with the three core components (insight, turning, and transformation), but the "dynamics of their conversion were quite different in comparison to the experience of Paul." With Paul it was an event: with the Twelve it was a process (106). Mark thus offers another model for conversion.

We can briefly summarize Peace's outline of Mark as follows. Mark, in his prologue (1:1-15) establishes the theme and vocabulary of conversion. Part I (1:16-8:30) describes the disciples' growth in understanding Jesus: as teacher, then prophet, then Messiah. In Part II (8:31-15:39) the disciples begin to discover just what kind of Messiah Jesus is: first Son of Man, then Son of David, then Son of God. In the epilogue (15:40-16:8) the death and resurrection both confirm their mature understanding of who Jesus is and provide a paradigm for conversion.

And he asked them,
"But who do you say that I am?"
Peter answered him,
"You are the Christ."
. . .
He rebuked Peter and said,
"Get behind me, Satan!
For you are not
setting your mind
on the things of God,
but on the things of man."
Mark 8:29, 33

The third section of the book begins with a critique of what Peace calls "encounter evangelism." He begins: "I have come to believe that how we conceive of conversion determines how we do evangelism" (286).

If our model is Paul we ask, "Will you receive Jesus as your Lord and Savior?" The assumption is that all people are interested and able to respond meaningfully. Events are arranged to promote such encounters.

If our model is the Twelve we ask, "Where are you on your spiritual pilgrimage and what issues are you wrestling with when it comes to God?" Here we are assuming that different people are at different places in their spiritual pilgrimage. Events are arranged that promote the process (small group Bible studies, seminars, conversations) (286).

Peace is not against encounter evangelism if it is done well. He writes:

> What we really need is the development of innovative ways of doing encounter evangelism that will reach the many people who are ready to encounter Christ while not alienating those who are still on the way (308).

But Peace does emphasize the notion of pilgrimage. And he includes a helpful description of the "geography" of spiritual pilgrimage (from quest, to commitment, to formation).

So how can we evaluate this contribution? Peace is to be applauded for returning to Scripture itself with his questions. He has widened the discussion of what constitutes a biblical conversion. Some, however, would contend that we need to probe the experience of Paul more deeply. For example Gordon Smith critiques Peace for too readily accepting Paul's conversion as a model conversion.[67] Is Peace still looking at Paul through the lens of the revivalist?

Then regarding Mark, the New Testament scholar Gundry has warned us about overly tidy analyses of Mark's Gospel.

---

[67] Gordon T. Smith, *Beginning Well: Christian Conversion & Authentic Transformation* (Downers Grove, IL: InterVarsity, 2001), p. 127.

This Gospel appears to have multiple layers and themes.[68] We wonder if Peace's outline fits too well.

Furthermore, if conversion is more process than event we are left with unanswered questions about boundary crossing. Is it possible to know if one is a Christian or not? If conversion can be such a lengthy process is there a broad middle ground when one is neither in nor out? (or both in and out?) To these questions we return later.

But we can be grateful for the discipline and passion Peace has brought to his subject. Peace has rightly moved the discussion around conversion away from Paul and into a broader arena. In so doing he has reduced the focus on conversion as *event* and credibly examined the biblical alternative of *process*. Should we not use the first apostles as examples of conversion at least as often as we use the later apostle? After all, the Lord Jesus personally oversaw the conversions of each of them.

b) George Hunter, *The Celtic Way of Evangelism: How Christianity Can Reach the West . . . Again* (Nashville, TN: Abingdon, 2001)

In this compelling study Hunter examines one of the less familiar trails in the history of the church and makes some surprising applications to this present age. Although he is speaking more broadly of evangelism he does bring a helpful perspective to conversion itself. Hunter sets the stage with the

---

[68] Robert H. Gundry, *Mark: A Commentary On His Apology For The Cross* (Grand Rapids, MI: Eerdmans, 1992).

story of St. Patrick. Patrick experienced a nominal Christian childhood in late fourth century England. He was kidnapped and sold into slavery in Ireland as a teenager, escaped after six years of hard labor and deepening faith, then returned to Ireland at age 48 as the first missionary bishop. He died about A.D. 460. In under 30 years God had used him to bring most of pagan Ireland to Christ.

This story is instructive for a number of reasons. There are some fascinating parallels between Patrick's world and ours. Firstly, by the time Patrick was born, Christendom was well established. Patrick himself began as a nominal Christian—one of the challenges of a Christendom environment, illustrating the way the church had already made a major shift from mission to maintenance.

Furthermore, whereas earlier Christians had brought Christ to the barbarians, now Christians felt people must be civilized (by which they meant Romanized) *before* they could be converted. In fact, as Hunter points out, "The British leaders were offended and angered that Patrick was spending priority time with 'pagans,' 'sinners,' and 'barbarians'" (24).[69] These Christendom problems began early! And though we are now living post-Christendom these same concerns linger still.

Secondly, Patrick was bringing Christianity to a barbarian land. Ireland had between 200,000 and 500,000 people in about 150 extended tribes. These folk were non-literate, community oriented, and close to nature. They loved story, visual art, songs, and symbols. They were accustomed to paradox and

---

[69] Beginning here the numbers in parenthesis are page numbers in Hunter.

mystery. They were in fact strikingly similar in their pre-modern world to post-moderns today.

England and Ireland were two very different worlds, yet Patrick was thoroughly at home in each. He was born into Christendom. But he had paid his dues in pagan Ireland with his six years of slavery. How many of us would be willing to enroll in such a school of missions? Will we who were born into Christendom have the courage to "dwell in another land" and learn to love that land as Patrick did? Perhaps it will be thrust upon us as it was upon Patrick. Of course for us that "other land" is not geographically distant, it is right here on our street.

A new commandment
I give to you,
that you love one another:
just as I have loved you,
you also are to love
one another.
By this all people will know
that you are my disciples,
if you have love for
one another.
John 13:34,35

Patrick's method of evangelism was to use a team of twelve or more including priests, students and women. They would set up camp alongside a settlement and live out their faith in community. They would pray for the sick, welcome visitors, look for ways to engage people in conversation, and give counsel. They used open-air speaking, combined with drama, song, and symbols. It was a wonderfully holistic, multi-dimensional form of evangelism. And it was effective.

By God's grace, the Irish were coming to faith. And what emerged was an indigenous church. A simple building was erected. A younger leader would remain. A few new believers would join the team as they moved to the next settlement. And so the fire spread.

What developed was not a parish church system but a series of what might be called monastic communities that offered not just centres of worship but a whole way of life. These were diverse, active, inclusive communities that incorporated children, schools, craftsmen and study as well as daily worship and regular prayer.

And, note this, from the beginning these communities were mission-oriented. Hunter writes,

> The Celtic Christian Movement proceeded to multiply mission-sending monastic communities, which continued to send teams into settlements to multiply churches and start people in the community-based life of full devotion to the Triune God (35).

This later extended beyond the natural boundaries of the island nation, to Iona and Scotland (A.D. 563), and then to Europe (A.D. 600).

But the tension between the Celtic way and the Roman way remained. Hunter points out that (compared to Roman Christianity) Celtic Christianity was:

- more movement than institution;
- its buildings were simple;
- there was more emphasis on imagination;
- it was less cerebral;
- it was closer to nature;
- it emphasized imminence and providence more than transcendence.

Another distinctive feature was the willingness to be indigenous. "They" didn't have to become like "us" before we could be brothers and sisters.

Eventually Celtic Christianity was largely pressed into the Roman mold (41). But it is a remarkable chapter in Christian history whose lessons remain.

Celtic evangelism was based on the premise that conversion takes time. The evangelistic outreach to a new settlement involved an extended period of interaction. Celtic evangelism worked through community. Whereas the Roman model (for those civilized enough) involved presentation, decision, *then* fellowship, the Celtic model established fellowship *first*. Then within this relationship unbelievers engaged in conversation, prayer, worship. As they discovered they believed, they were invited to commit (53). "The Celtic model reflects the adage that, for most people, 'Christianity is more caught than taught.'" (54).

Hunter argues that for post-modern people, coming to faith *gradually* (the Celtic model) is more common than coming to faith *suddenly* (the Roman model) (54). "Evangelism is now about helping people to belong so that they can believe" (55).

Was Celtic Christianity all good news?—no. As Hunter points out (89), it was too optimistic about human nature. It would have benefited from a Celtic Augustine to paint the true depths of human sin. It over-emphasized divine imminence at the expense of divine transcendence. Its eagerness to be indigenous could fall over into syncretism. Its enthusiasm to pray through every aspect of daily life could degenerate into formulas that were more like pagan incantations.

But there was so much that was good. Celtic Christianity still speaks to our day, the day of the New Barbarians who also inhabit a mysterious, paradoxical, tribal, multi-sensory world. If we think these new pilgrims are unconvertible (as the Roman church did the Irish) perhaps we should, like Patrick, re-examine our assumptions about conversion.

c) **Robert Webber,** *Journey to Jesus: The Worship, Evangelism and Nurture Mission of the Church* **(Nashville, TN: Abingdon, 2001)**

The story of Patrick may illustrate some of the weaknesses already evident in the early western church, but Robert Webber reminds us there is still much good to be gleaned from the early history of the church. In this study he takes us to Rome, to the centrepoint of the Christian West. But he also takes us back to an earlier time—before Patrick, to a pre-Christendom time, a time when the church was still very much a minority presence.

Webber is passionate about promoting the treasures of the early church and has written much in this area. His argument in *Journey to Jesus* is that the early church has a lot to teach us about the conversion process and how the church can nurture that process. His primary source material is *The Apostolic Tradition* (A.D. 215) by Hippolytus (Bishop of Rome).

Webber is clear up front that he is not interested in merely presenting another academic study. He is looking for practical help for people coming to faith. "How can we take the longing so many people have for spiritual fulfillment and connect it with the Christian tradition of faith and spirituality?" (10).[70]

The Apostolic Tradition describes a four stage model of evangelism that led to full incorporation into the church. The ancient names for each stage were: Seeker, Hearer, Kneeler, and Faithful. Between each were three rites of passage, the most significant being the rite of baptism leading to the Faithful entering into the full life of the church. Conversion in the early church was thus both *process* oriented and *church* oriented, "not a one-time decision made without a support community" (11).

Webber (like Hunter) notes the current emergence of a neo-pagan world (18), a situation deeply troubling to the present-day church. The early church was also formed in a pagan and hostile environment. But it was convinced that God was at work in the world rescuing the world from the powers of evil through Jesus Christ (19). The church both a) bore witness to the mission of God (20), and b) "embodied God's future redemption" (36).

Thus conversion in the early church meant a radical realignment of allegiance—from the powers of evil to Christ. He notes:

> It was an evangelism with teeth, not an "easy believism" or a "cheap grace"; and it was a spiritual journey of discipleship, spiritual formation, and entrance into a new community (42).

Webber summarizes four themes in all this: warfare (*Christus Victor*); nurturing (church as mother); conversion as

---

[70] Beginning here the numbers in parentheses are page numbers in Webber.

process; and the importance of performative symbol. He argues that with the collapse of Christendom the church urgently needs to rediscover its missional character. "The church . . . not only has a story to tell but is itself the reality and embodiment of the story" (47). So the very process of conversion, which is the path of entry into the new community, is itself standing in witness to God's mission.

Webber sees in the early church a clear community-orientation to evangelism. Evangelism is not the work of one or two gifted people, it proceeds from the life of a missional congregation. There is both a personal and corporate witness to Christ. This underlines the need for renewal in the congregation because: "In the post-modern form of witness we bring people to Christ through the church. The church is the doorway to Christ" (70).

Individuals share their enthusiasm for the Christian community with the people in their network of relationships. They are not saying, "Here are four things you need to believe," but, "Come and see this community that has changed my life" (73). "The Christian brings the unchurched to a healthy, vibrant community of faith and, through association with an embodied community, faith is discerned and caught as the Gospel is overheard" (74).

The four stage entry model gave new believers the benefit of a guided pathway through a remarkable period of transition. Webber quotes Origen who noted that in contrast to the philosophers of the day, Christians had an organized way of leading people to maturity, and thus were more effective (83).

As the new pilgrims travel greater distances to faith in our own neo-pagan environment we do well to rethink paths of entry. We do no service by making the journey too short or too simple. Webber notes:

> It takes time for pagans to enter this new community—time for formation, time for the acquisition of new values, time for the transfer of allegiance from world powers to the power of Christ working through his body, the Church (97).

So the Seeker became the Hearer. The Hearer participated in the worship service, but left for specialized teaching during the Eucharist. In this way the Hearer grew through both teaching and involvement in the church community. Then, upon examination, the Hearer would advance to the Kneeler stage.

The shift from Hearer to Kneeler indicates the deepening spirituality. It is here that the battle with evil dominates. The battle is not fought alone however, but in the context of the community. There were various prayers for cleansing. Then there was the formal presentation of the Apostles' Creed and the Lord's Prayer, both to be memorized. In the Creed and the Prayer, Kneelers were being entrusted with the heart of the Gospel (138).

The Kneeler stage would be timed to coincide with Lent. This led to Easter baptism, the first Eucharist, and incorporation into

Everyone then who hears these words of mine and does them will be like a wise man who built his house on the rock. And the rain fell, and the floods came, and the winds blew and beat on that house, but it did not fall, because it had been founded on the rock.

Matthew 7:24, 25

the church as full members. Often the newly baptized would wear the white gowns for a whole week, receiving the Eucharist daily. It was a powerful, visible, missional expression during a time when Christians commonly died for their faith.

And so began the journey of the Faithful. Instruction continued. Gifts were discerned. "An essential aspect of spiritual integration into the community is in helping the Faithful discover the gift God has given them in ministry"(177). The Faithful were taught to have concern, not just for the church, but for the world. This was about more than just "saving souls" it included the "cultural mandate" (Genesis 1 and 2). "Each member of the church should see his or her calling in life to live and work in the world in such a way that the real truth about the world is made evident" (179).

Webber's portrayal of the carefully thought-through process of evangelism in the early church comes to us as a challenge. How do our pathways of initiation compare? This is not about making it difficult to join, this is about doing our best to see that new believers begin well. Throughout the book Webber suggests application for the present. He challenges us to rework this process for our churches today.

Do I have concerns about any of this?—yes. Firstly, there is the practicality of incorporating such a year-long program into the life of the church and into the lives of hyperactive 21st century people. One of the realities of our time and place is the complexity and diversity of people's lives and schedules. In my pastoral experience it has been difficult enough to get people to attend all four of the two-hour sessions we used for baptism and membership preparation (which some people solemnly informed me were far too onerous, and others, with equal solemnity, informed me were far too shallow.)

Then again, the convenience of squeezing people into a standardized format must be weighed against the need for a true spirit of hospitality in an age of fragmentation and discontinuity. There just isn't a "one-size-fits-all" doorway into the church.

My second concern is in regard to a particular inconsistency between Webber's historical analysis and his present-day application. He describes the ancient rite of passage from Seeker (phase 1) to Hearer (phase 2) as the rite of "welcome." But when he translates this into suggestions for current practice he re-labels this rite "conversion" (e.g. 26). This is confusing since at other times he refers to the entire process as conversion (e.g. 64). In fact this *process* orientation to conversion is a key emphases of the book. By choosing to name that particular rite "conversion" Webber unnecessarily raises questions about the nature of the rest of the process. What precisely is conversion? When does it occur? Is each part of the process equally important? And, if we are going to label only one part of the process conversion, why not choose baptism?

Nevertheless this is a profound book that makes a valuable contribution to the discussion. It may come as a shock to us in our time to discover such a thoughtful and thorough process of entry already functioning in the earliest years of the church. Thank God that the fading of modernity has made it easier for us to value and appreciate the best of the past and incorporate it into our present day church life.

d) Gordon Smith, *Beginning Well: Christian Conversion and Authentic Transformation* (Downers Grove, IL: InterVarsity, 2001).

Gordon Smith is very helpful to us at this point in the discussion because of his ability to link tradition, Scripture and present experience in a way that provides a satisfying map of conversion. He has a heart for church renewal; however, he is convinced this "will not come through efforts to foster revival but through a renewed appreciation and formulation of the nature of conversion" (24).[71] Smith is concerned that, although conversion is one of the four pillars of evangelicalism (Bebbington again), evangelicals have a shallow understanding of conversion that does not adequately account for its complexity (or the complexity of human religious experience more generally). He writes:

> Many Christians have anemic spiritual lives with little freedom, little growth in grace, and little commitment to obedience and service. I propose that an appropriate response to this predicament includes facing up to the fact that the church has a weak notion of conversion. True conversion leads to growth, commitment and service (24f.).

Smith helpfully addresses the tension between conversion as event and conversion as process. This is not just an academic debate. We experience the tension personally as we recognize process in our own conversion and at the same time long for clarity—a bench-mark boundary crossing.

---

[71] Beginning here the numbers in parentheses are page numbers in Gordon Smith.

Here the contrast between "bounded sets" and "centred sets" is instructive (36f.). Bounded sets focus on identity (an item is either an apple or not); centred sets focus on relationship (where the item is, in relation to the centre).

The climate of modernity, with its addiction both to certain knowledge and individualism, naturally fostered a leaning to the bounded-set view of conversion (as we saw above in revivalism). But the centred-set version is now more attractive to post-moderns who are more relational (even tribal) and who revel in ambiguity, mystery and pilgrimage, and who reject rigid definitions (particularly of themselves).

Smith feels that some sort of boundary is essential, but the centred-set approach rightly puts the focus on the centre (37). Smith argues that the church cannot in any case precisely determine the boundary between faith and non-faith, neither is the church called to be the manager of this boundary (38). The church is called to lift up Christ who is the centre.

So Smith (like Hunter and Webber) emphasizes the role of community in conversion. He discusses, for example, the importance of language in human experience. Religious experience also needs language to give it definition and clarity. But language requires community. Thus religious experience (including conversion) is shaped by language learned in community (which is a process). This is one reason why so many of us need to belong before we believe. We need to learn the language of faith that can foster and give expression to our conversion (42).

Smith challenges us to learn the language of faith not only from our immediate church setting, but also from the larger church, present and past. He uses conversion narratives of four very different people (Augustine, Ignatius Loyola, John Wesley, and Dorothy Day) to broaden the debate. He notes the complexity of their experience: none of these conversions was the result of preaching for a decision; many people were involved in bringing these people to faith; and each conversion was "protracted rather than punctiliar" (76f.).

Smith also challenges us to thoughtfully and honestly write out our own conversion narrative as a way of understanding and owning the unique working of God's grace in our own lives. This is a helpful reminder to us post-moderns that individuality is not lost in community but in fact finds voice and definition in community.

American evangelicalism has been very influential in the past century both in North America and through American missions around the world. But it is important to reflect on how this strand of Christianity was formed. Smith points out that conversion, in this movement, "has been shaped largely by revivalism and crusade evangelism" (80).

He then steps back to identify three "classic perspectives" on conversion. First the Benedictine (Roman Catholic) tradition: "Conversion as a decision to join a community that is seeking salvation" (thus the strength of *spiritual formation* in that tradition) (81). Second the Reformed tradition: Conversion as a "once-for-all experience, past tense" (thus the emphasis on, and possibility of, *assurance*) (82). The danger of the first is a tendency to works righteousness. The danger of the second is that the goal of conversion, transformation, is often neglected. Third the Holiness tradition: conversion is a one-time event, but is followed by a further *sanctifying work of the Spirit*. The danger here is the creation of a two-tiered Christian community (those who have the second experience, and those who don't.)

Smith traces the development of the Reformation strand through the Puritans, Jonathan Edwards, and John Wesley. But he is particularly concerned with the pervasive influence of Charles Finney in the early 19th century. Smith writes: "Many if not most evangelicals are unwitting children of the movement, associating the language and piety in revivalism with the New Testament" (94).

Some of his concerns include: over-emphasis on the will and neglect of the mind; over-simplification and standardization; over-valuing the dramatic; under valuing spiritual disciplines; no notion of sacrament; and the privatization of religion and downplaying of community (93f.). Thus we find ourselves at the beginning of the 21st century "alienated from our own experience" and without a meaningful theology of conversion (100). And, we might add, quite unprepared to foster conversions in the new post-everything world.

> *Therefore, as you received*
> *Christ Jesus the Lord,*
> *so walk in him,*
> *rooted and built up in him*
> *and established in the faith,*
> *just as you were taught,*
> *abounding in thanksgiving.*
> Colossians 2:6, 7

Smith now turns to Scripture with fresh inquiry. From a survey of the Synoptics, Acts, Paul and John, he distills seven conversion elements. All of these components, he now argues, are necessary as a foundation for a transformed life:

- belief in Jesus
- repentance
- trust in Jesus
- transfer of allegiance
- baptism
- receiving the gift of the Spirit
- incorporation into congregational life.

These are to be thought of as a cluster (not as steps—the order varies for different people). Belief and repentance form the core of conversion but not the whole. This is critical because spiritual immaturity and poor growth result from over emphasizing one or two elements to the neglect of the others. Though we may have differing entry points, "eventually, for a person to be fully converted and have a good foundation for a continued experience of the transforming grace of God, all seven elements need to be encountered and experienced" (147).

It is beyond the scope of this study to pursue further Smith's subsequent exploration of these elements. But this introduction indicates the relevance of Smith's work for our time.

In taking seriously the complexity of conversion Smith helps us understand better the event/process tension. Conversion is God's deep, mysterious, gracious work. He is not in a hurry. Some elements may be cataclysmic, others will be unpacked slowly. Surely we see here God respecting the uniqueness of each woman and man as he calls us back to himself.

Smith helps us understand better the tension between individual and community. God works incarnationally through social and cultural contexts. The church is to be the midwife of conversion—an evangelistic community that gives space for each individual.

Smith also helps us understand the diversity of conversion experience. There is a broad pattern, but within the pattern there are endless variations of emphasis, timing and shape. This allows us to continue an evangelical focus on conversion, but with humility (we are not the managers), expecting the unexpected (His ways are not always our ways), and alert for Love's creativity (He is still not willing that any should perish.)

Summary

I have chosen these four authors because of the relevance of their work to Christian conversion in the 21st century.

Peace goes directly to Scripture with his concerns about event versus process. His analysis of Mark provides biblical warrant for the journey paradigm.

Hunter looks to the historical model of evangelism in Ireland to illustrate the complexity of the journey from paganism to mature Christian faith. He highlights the role of the evangelistic community, the importance of inclusion

For no one can lay a foundation other than that which is laid, which is Jesus Christ. Now if anyone builds on the foundation with gold, silver, precious stones, wood, hay, straw— each one's work will become manifest, for the Day will disclose it, because it will be revealed by fire . . .

1 Corinthians 3:11-13

before belief, and the power of non-cerebral elements (story, song, symbol) in winning non-Christendom people to Christ.

Webber looks back even further, to the early church's deliberate and careful process of leading people from unbelief to spiritual maturity. He emphasizes the necessity of church, the importance of disciplined teaching, the power of symbolic rite, and the importance of faith lived out holistically.

Smith weaves together experience, tradition and Scripture to display the wonder and complexity of conversion. The church in recent history has minimized conversion. Smith argues that we need to rediscover the full meaning of a "good beginning" if we are to see the kind of substantial and ongoing transformation expected in biblical Christianity.

Midscript

(Nicodemus in process)

The officers then came to the chief priests and Pharisees, who said to them, "Why did you not bring him?" [46]The officers answered, "No one ever spoke like this man!" [47]The Pharisees answered them, "Have you also been deceived? [48]Have any of the authorities or the Pharisees believed in him? [49]But this crowd that does not know the law is accursed." [50]Nicodemus, who had gone to him before, and who was one of them, said to them, [51]"Does our law judge a man without first giving him a hearing and learning what he does?" [52]They replied, "Are you from Galilee too? Search and see that no prophet arises from Galilee."

John 7:45-52

3. New Approaches To Conversion

Evangelicalism will continue as a significant force for Christianity into the foreseeable future. Its four-pillar approach has proven robust enough to navigate the choppy seas of the closing days of the last millennium and is already rising to the challenge of this new age. But there will need to be adjustments, particularly to that pillar we call conversionism, if evangelicalism is to sustain its vitality. Here I suggest four movements necessary for this renewal, movements that are, I believe, already underway.

a) From Decisions To Conversions

Dateable decisions may have been an understandable concern in the age of Christendom, blighted as it was with the scourge of nominality. When everyone was, in some sense, a Christian, a datable decision to follow Jesus personally was helpful evidence of authentic faith. But unfortunately, as we have seen, decisionism was too aligned with the spirit of modernity to be either spiritually healthy or of lasting value. Now, in our post-modern environment, the mindset that nurtured a focus on decision has faded. And with the expiring of Christendom the problem of nominality is also greatly diminished. Only someone serious about spiritual matters would claim to be a Christian in this new environment. It is time to move the focus from decision to conversion.

This, of course, is where it always should have been. Smith has clearly demonstrated conversion to be much broader than decision. But beside the theological rationale there is also a sociological and psychological rationale. A clear decision may have satisfied a desire to secure heaven. But, as Schaller notes, "People today are concerned with 'identity goals' rather than 'survival goals.'"[72] And it takes much more than a decision to secure identity. Identity emerges as people grow in relationship to Christ and to the people of Christ. We need a relational conversion.

But you are a chosen race, a royal priesthood, a holy nation, a people for his own possession, that you may proclaim the excellencies of him who called you out of darkness into his marvelous light. Once you were not a people, but now you are God's people

1 Peter 2:9, 10

We are discovering that today's generation is not asking what must I do to be saved, but what must I do to be loved?[73] This love-hunger will only be satisfied by a conversion that encompasses much more than making a decision. So we see that, given the experiential orientation of today's emerging generations, the affective aspects of conversion will often precede the volitional.

---

[72] Schaller quoted by Chuck Smith, p. 145.
[73] Flory, p. 1.

Webber persuasively argues that post-modern evangelism needs to relearn a holistic approach that includes: Christ's victory over evil; radical obedience to Christ; and the conversion of both vertical and horizontal relationships. "Post-modern evangelism not only announces the kingdom but also seeks to inaugurate the kingdom in the biblical sense."[74] And inaugurating the kingdom demands a holistic conversion.

The focus on decisions may have helped us manage the evangelistic process. But we must now learn to be mentors, not managers. It is time to acknowledge the greater ambiguity of a multi-faceted conversion that includes, to use Smith's categories: belief, penitence, trust, volition, baptism, Spirit-filling, and community-commitment. At the same time recognizing and respecting the uniqueness, the *what-is-that-to-thee-ness* (see John 21:22), of each person's unique walk with our Lord.

b) From Membership To Pilgrimage

If the concern with decisionism lies in the over-simplification of the complexity of conversion, the concern with membership lies in the collapsing of process into event. Where membership is a high priority, conversion is more likely to be viewed primarily as the boundary crossing, thus leading to an undue equating of conversion with an event that permits membership. The centred set approach discussed earlier is a corrective. Here, the focus is on Christ and away from the boundary, and the emphasis shifts from membership to pilgrimage.

---

[74] Webber, p. 150f.

Growing churches need to be intentional about incorporating new believers, this is an important element of their conversion. But there is, rightly, a concern that large churches, in particular, may focus on moving people into deeper *institutional* commitment rather than into a deeper *relational* commitment—a deeper experience of community.[75] Membership will still play a role in churches large and small, but it will be more about relationship and function than institutional growth. Can we have the same shyness about counting heads that David came to have (2 Samuel 24)?

Furthermore, one of the characteristics of the emerging church paradigm is the ambiguous nature of the boundary to the congregation. Churches will need to accept an increasing level of untidiness as conversion becomes less predictable and often prolonged. The new pilgrims may be active and serving in the name of Christ even before they have really come to terms with who Christ is. Others may be clearly devoted to Christ but leery of the institution. It may be more helpful for the church to put up with a messy boundary and focus on pilgrimage than to persist in categorizing people. We remember that membership is not a *destination* but a *doorway* to deeper discipleship and ministry.[76] (The new pilgrims already know this!)

The focus on pilgrimage is not just of concern for those entering the faith, it is also of concern for long time members. Pilgrimage is movement, it is a sign of life. We actively join with God as he calls onward the faithful remnant.[77] This has

---

[75] Chuck Smith, p. 185.
[76] Schaller 1995, p. 26.
[77] Gibbs 2000, p. 41.

always been so. Perhaps what is new for us now is the prevalence of these metaphors of process—"journey," "walk," "pilgrimage," "voyage," "passage," and so on.[78]

The millennial project of Christ Church Cathedral (Anglican) in Victoria, B.C., was the construction of a labyrinth. This ancient concept of a maze-like circular pathway has re-emerged in the post-modern world (yet another illustration of a rediscovered past.) The practice of walking and meditating your way through a labyrinth provides a visual, bodily experience that resonates with today's "quest culture." But the spirit of the labyrinth must move from the lawn to the lobby and into the sanctuary.

The move from membership to pilgrimage is especially helpful to many GenXers and Millennials who live with a fragmented identity and so may never be able to relate fully to a once-and-for-all conversion experience. Many women and men of these younger generations begin each day-dawn asking again, "Who am I? Tell me again, what does it all mean?" A pilgrimage orientation allows and encourages these wanderers to claim each day for Christ.[79]

I remember my affliction and my wanderings . . .

But this I call to mind, and therefore I have hope: The steadfast love of the LORD never ceases; his mercies never come to an end; they are new every morning; great is your faithfulness. "The LORD is my portion," says my soul, "therefore I will hope in him."

Lamentations 3:19-24

---

[78] Roof, p. 46.
[79] Beaudoin, p. 173.

Pilgrimage is really about ongoing spiritual formation. How do we relearn what this means and how do we nurture it? We may need to look across to the Roman Catholic wing of the church for help here. Certainly we must look beyond the "ten easy steps" approach produced in the dying days of modernity. As McGrath notes, growth often comes very slowly, and often not without much sorrow and suffering.[80]

Thomas Oden comments on the expanded vista of our present age:

> Long-set-aside possibilities and aptitudes for spiritual formation are at long last now viable which have had a prolonged history of being disdained by modernity. We are thinking here of sexual purity, covenant fidelity, the wonderful privilege of parenting, the rediscovery of providence in history, and the grace to reason morally out of the premise of revelation.[81]

Symbol and sacrament will recover their place of honor in churches that have moved their focus from membership to pilgrimage, The bread and the wine harken back, through the cross, to the Passover—the preparation for the desert journey. And later, looking over our shoulders, we will discover that, somewhere along the way, we crossed a boundary.

---

[80] McGrath, p. 52.
[81] Thomas C. Oden, "So What Happens After Modernity? A Postmodern Agenda For Evangelical Theology," in Dockery, p. 185.

c) From Soul-Winner To Evangelistic Community

The evangelistic paradigm for the church in modernity was the soul-winner. The soul-winner model highlighted the evangelism-gifted individual, the human agency of salvation, and the event-ness of conversion. In contrast, I suggest, the evangelistic paradigm for the church in post-modernity is the evangelistic community. This model emphasizes relationship, worship and journey. As Webber argues:

> People in a post-modern world are not persuaded to faith by reason as much as they are moved to faith by participation in God's earthly community.[82]

Christian love has always found expression in hospitality. Now, in our increasingly fragmented world, congregational hospitality is, more than ever, a powerful evangelistic force. To be truly hospitable means to welcome warmly, to make someone feel at home, and to respect and appreciate the new-comer. Thomas Frank is describing the spirit of hospitality when he writes: "Congregations help people find their place, encourage them to make a place, and comfort them when they do not fit a place."[83] The hospitable church is willing to provide a home for the unbeliever. This corporate expression of love prepares the unbeliever for the hospitality of Christ.

This renewed emphasis on the evangelistic potential of a welcoming community is good news for those who suffer more from shame than guilt. Shame is a relational problem and

---

[82] Webber, p. 79.
[83] Thomas E. Frank, *The Soul of the Congregation: An Invitation to Congregational Reflection* (Nashville, TN: Abingdon Press, 2000) p. 20.

requires a relational response.[84] An impersonal presentation of an abstract solution will not touch the hearts of the shamed.

The church that is willing to move beyond merely supplying accommodation, to providing true hospitality, will keep on stretching and growing. An environment of hospitality nurtures not only the conversion of the unbeliever but also the ongoing conversion of the church itself. In the global village the "locals" will learn to welcome the "cosmopolitans."[85] Mono-cultural congregations will become multi-cultural and multi-coloured, and be led by multi-lingual pastors in cross-ethnic marriages!

We are told that part of the appeal of Islam to African Americans is the racial inclusiveness and the emphasis on community (the *ummah*).[86] But this inclusiveness was written into Christian DNA from the very birthday of the church (long before the birth of Islam). On the day of Pentecost people from 15 different countries and regions gathered in Jerusalem to be surprised by the dramatic outpouring of the Spirit and the compelling preaching of the Gospel (Acts 2). Should not the followers of Jesus still be leading the way in responding to this longing of the nations to be included?

But this is not just about racial loneliness. This shift from the individual to the community in evangelistic effectiveness is shaped by a renewed importance and appreciation of relationship all across society. Relationship has replaced reason as an organizing principle in our new world,[87] not least, because GenXers and Millennials (in contrast to Boomers)

---

[84] Forrester, p. 230f.
[85] Ibid., p. 142.
[86] Gibbs 2000, p. 201.
[87] Schaller 1995, p. 15.

place a high value on authentic community. It is a way of making up for the social breakdown in family and community life that has been so much a part of their experience.[88] Statistics Canada reports that by 2011 there were more single-parent households with children, than couple households with children. People are hungry for a place to call home.

The church is at her most hospitable and most evangelistic when she invites the new pilgrim to participate in the very act of worship. This, of course, is not a new concept. From early days the church at worship has powerfully impacted unbelievers. Under Christendom the impact diminished. But in a post-Christendom world, the church at worship is once again counter-cultural, or better, is establishing and practicing her own radically different Kingdom culture. (Clapp points out that the word culture derives, in part, from "cultus," worship.[89])

In worship we practice and participate in an alternate reality. We see the way God sees. We live and relate according to alternate rules. In worship the unbeliever sees the church at her most intimate and vulnerable moment,

If, therefore, the whole church comes together and all speak in tongues, and outsiders or unbelievers enter, will they not say that you are out of your minds?
But if all prophesy, and an unbeliever or outsider enters, he is convicted by all, he is called to account by all, the secrets of his heart are disclosed, and so, falling on his face, he will worship God and declare that God is really among you.

1 Corinthians 14:23-25

---

[88] Flory, p. 2.
[89] Clapp, pp. 66, 98f.

her most authentic moment. We may be surprised at how much the pagan understands of that moment. We may be startled by the reverence of the pagan in worship. They are "yearning for the mysterious transcendence."[90] They may even show more reverence than the faithful!

Should the worship service be altered to accommodate the non-believer? Only to remove obvious hindrances such as excessive archaisms, obscure insider church jargon, sexist language, "good enough" standards (rather than excellence)—all of which need to be changed in any case. What is needed in worship is true worship. For some this will require doing less and being still more. As Guinness comments:

> "Precisely because the Gospel carries the oxygen of eternity, it allows modern people to catch their breath as they pant breathlessly toward their temporal goals." [91]

For others this will require more opportunity to respond and engage.

True worship is not boring, neither for believers nor unbelievers. Evangelism is our natural response to an encounter with the divine (see Luke 24:33f., John 1:45). In true worship people meet the Lord and naturally want to go out and talk about him. But the worship experience itself is also a living witness to the Gospel. And unbelievers can be welcomed to the occasion.

To what extent should unbelievers participate in worship? We may be surprised to hear that John Wesley even invited seekers to participate at the Communion Table. Hunter writes,

---

[90] Gibbs 2001, p. 156.
[91] Guinness, p. 64.

"He saw the Eucharist as a 'converting ordinance'"—as a place where unbelievers might discover the grace of God.[92] After all, did Jesus not serve the unbelieving and the doubting at that first Communion service? If we are uncomfortable with actually including the unbeliever at the family meal, at least we can so celebrate the occasion that, as Smith writes, "The person standing at the periphery of the church will say, 'All this talk of food is making me hungry,' and, 'All this talk of family is making me homesick.'" And so the prodigal will be compelled to return to the Father's house.[93]

A strong ministry of the Word is essential to the effectiveness of the evangelistic community. First of all because churches need to proclaim, in words, vigorously and clearly, the Gospel of Jesus Christ. But secondly because that Word is heard best *in community*. Good though it is, there are limitations to the private, silent reading of Scripture. The Word of God is intended for corporate reading and listening—it is meant to be heard aloud, and lived out, together.[94]

The ministry of the Word occurs most profoundly in the context of the people of God at worship. The gathered faithful hear the heart of God, in the words of God, through the fragile messenger. And the gathered unfaithful eavesdrop. The Word cannot to be disengaged from time and place and context, but is made flesh again in the body of Christ, which is his church. And so the church becomes Immanuel ("God with us") for the unbeliever.

---

[92] Hunter, p. 166.
[93] Chuck Smith, p. 139.
[94] Clapp, p. 127.

So for the 90% of pastors who do not have the gift of evangelism, and are re-considering their calling in a post-Christendom world, a better alternative to resigning is learning to nurture the church as an evangelistic community. Perhaps it is better if pastors *don't* have a special gift for evangelism! Then they are more likely to strive to evoke the gift of evangelism in the community of faith—where it really belongs.

Yet pastors can model an evangelistic presence—gift or no gift. They can be deliberate about keeping connected with the non-church world, for starters. Why not move out of the gated community and into an "at risk" community? or into the middle of an immigrant neighbourhood? Or why not shop at the mom and pop stores instead of the impersonal chains?—and get to know the moms and pops.

At the beginning of the third millennium, churches are being called to retake their position front and centre in the evangelistic endeavor. The new pilgrims (though they may not know it yet) are hungry for this. Post-modern conversions need the time, the acceptance, the hermeneutical environment, and the sense of an imminent, Holy God that a community of faith provides.

d) From Parish Church To Missional Church

The need to move the focus from soul-winner to evangelistic community results from the recovery of the importance of relationship and process in the wake of the departure of modernity. The shift from parish church to missional church is a broader concept that results from the departure of

Christendom. The first step in nurturing converts is to accept that our neighbours need converting.

It might once have been adequate to focus mission efforts beyond the frontiers of Christendom in some distant land. And there is still a need for evangelistic work in distant lands. But that frontier now begins at the threshold of the church (if not inside the church itself). This calls for a dramatic shift in the practice of church and in the mindset behind the practice.

It is no small matter to move from being a "church with a mission, to being a missional church"[95]—from meeting the *ministry* demands of a church culture to addressing the *missionary* demands of an unchurched culture.[96] Consider, for example, that as Christendom recedes satanic activity becomes more overt. Frontier missionaries have always been alert to spiritual power-encounters. But how will long-settled churches respond to these kinds of challenges? It will feel as though we have been parachuted into a foreign land. Will we have the spirit of adventure and creativity demanded of us as we engage this neo-pagan world?

One option is to die as the old Christendom pipeline of new members dries up. Another option is to change. But (as Regele argues) the depth of change required may make the way forward seem like death in any case![97] Agents of change will need to help the church process the grief (as we saw earlier, through shock, denial, anger, bargaining, depression, then on to acceptance and renewed hope). Trained, transitional pastors will be a hot commodity. Churches resolved to engage in the

[95] Darrell L. Guder ed., *Missional Church: A Vision for the Sending of the Church in North America* (Grand Rapids, MI: Eerdmans, 1998), p. 6.
[96] Gibbs 2000, p. 98.
[97] Regele, p. 240.

task of converting the unconverted will begin with their own conversion. As Smith writes, "The world is not going to be changed by Christians who merely go to church."[98] But it will be in the practice of calling others to conversion that the church enters most deeply into her own conversion.

The conversion from parish church to missional church may not begin with the leaders (change is often initiated at the fringe) but eventually it must be adopted by the leaders. Pastors who signed up for chaplaincy roles may baulk at missionary work. They may not be equipped sociologically, culturally, linguistically, or gastronomically(!) for cross-cultural mission. Nevertheless, missional churches require a mission mind-set at the helm.

Somehow it is easier to be a mission presence in an exotic far off land, with its constant cultural and linguistic challenges to remind us. But it requires a steely resolve and torrents of grace for churches and their leaders to develop and sustain a missional stance while remaining geographically at home. Christendom addictions die hard. (It is an exercise that will deepen our empathy with the dry alcoholic who must pass the liquor store on the way to work every day.) It will certainly be easier for the pastor to write about the missional life than engage in it!

In the transition from *parishional* to *missional* the church must re-evaluate its relation to the world around. The old dictum about being "in the world but not of the world" takes on a new edge when the welcome mat is gone. The church must relearn what it means to dwell in the world, as a distinct

---

[98] Chuck Smith, p. 184.

culture, as a distinct way of life, neither incorporating uncritically the world's values, nor living in isolation, but continually reassessing what it means to follow the Spirit in each generation.[99] The antidote to *incorporation* is a heart set on things above (a robust eschatology); the antidote to *isolation* is a heart that breaks for the last, the least and the lost.

Missional churches will not be so attached to their old (or new) buildings. They will be quicker to remodel, or relocate, if that aids the mission. The mission budget will no longer be one hard-fought slice of the overall budget, the *whole* church budget will be the mission budget.

Missional churches will broker friendships between uneasy ethnic communities. They will engage in practical, hands on, economic development for people on the margins. They will establish contagious outposts of shalom in volatile neighbourhoods.

If indeed we are entering the age of the New Barbarian (fueled in part by the breakdown of families and social structures) missional churches may again be called on to provide basic education as past missions once did. Similarly, as health costs exceed the grasp of increasing numbers of people, medical missions may be needed much closer to home than they have been in the recent past. Many churches now have a Parish Nurse (but they need a better title!) It is this kind of reformulated presence in the neighbourhood that will alert the unconverted to the possibilities of grace.

Some observers are worried that "missional" will turn out to mean "market-oriented." This has proven to be a valid

---

[99] Clapp, p. 140f.

concern as some churches and movements have been seduced by marketplace concepts of growth, usefulness, competition, and "exchange" (displacing grace).[100] But that approach was, in part, a child of now floundering modernity, and is thus losing its appeal. If market-oriented means a greater sensitivity to the unchurched, all well and good. It may even be that in some corners the concern over "marketing" is a red herring. As Schaller argues, "The real issue is not consumerism. It is the threat of changes brought by people 'who are not like us.'"[101]

The fact is, to be missional means to be much more accommodating to outsiders. (This includes tolerating the smell of strange food cooking in the church kitchen!) And until we actually engage in the process and begin to welcome the "other" we will probably still under-estimate Regele's dictum that the church must die before it can live.

Have no fear of them, nor be troubled, but in your hearts honor Christ the Lord as holy, always being prepared to make a defense to anyone who asks you for a reason for the hope that is in you; yet do it with gentleness and respect, having a good conscience, so that, when you are slandered, those who revile your good behavior in Christ may be put to shame.

1 Peter 3:14-16

As the newly-missional church becomes serious about converting the unconverted in a post-Christendom milieu, it is thrown back into an old dilemma. Two scandals hinder the unbeliever from turning to Christ. One is the messenger. The other is the message.[102] The message of the Gospel will always be an

---

[100] Frank, p. 29f.
[101] Schaller 1995, p. 79.
[102] Erickson, p. 308.

offense—it is an offense to human pride, we resist bowing the knee to grace. But the offense of the messenger is another matter. Missional churches are willing to do what it takes to reduce offense of the messenger without diminishing the offence of the Gospel.

What will that take? We can begin with a less strident tone as we present our Christian Grand Story—a greater modesty. We can show more respect by no longer assuming others will know our religious language and church culture. We can major on the *reconciliation* Christ makes possible, rather than on *separation* from this or that. That will make a beginning.

The move from parish church to missional church is critical if the unconverted are to be converted. Where else will new members come from in a post-Christendom world? For some churches this will mean learning a whole new language, the very language of conversion is foreign to them. In the chaplaincy role of Christendom, conversion was not even in the job description—converted from what?

One elderly minister said she had only recently discovered the vocabulary necessary to speak clearly about conversion (though she is converted!) Does she have a low IQ? Has she neglected the Scriptures?—no. She is simply a child of her age.

But this is no time to be pointing fingers. There will be surprises and challenges for all churches as we come to terms with the culture shock of waking up in a mission field.

Summary

So we have begun to accept that we inhabit a profoundly changed environment. And we have begun to think about the implications of this for Christian conversion. What kinds of responses are now emerging?

First we see the shift away from "decisions." This is a move from simplicity to complexity, from event to process. Certainly this means that conversions will be harder to track (and harder to manage). But it also turns out to be more in touch with reality, and so opens the door to conversions that are deeper, and subsequent transformations that are more profound.

Related to this is the move from membership to pilgrimage. Complex and thorough conversions need time. With the focus off the boundary and on Christ, conversions find breathing room. Not only are new believers encouraged to make their pursuit of Christ life-long, but older sedentary pilgrims are swept up into the procession.

With the spotlight moving off the "soul-winner" and onto the "evangelistic congregation," evangelicalism provides early signs of its recovery from the addictions of modernity, in particular modernity's obsession with individualism. The concept of the evangelistic community underscores the importance of relationship, belonging, even language itself, that is only really possible in community. Here the new pilgrim can "taste and see that the Lord is good" in the supportive company of those who already know.

What is needed is a conversion of the church itself—from parish church to missional church. And a "decision" at this point is not enough! A thorough conversion is needed here too.

It begins with honestly accepting that our near neighbours need to meet Christ also, followed by a willingness to do what it takes to see that happen. It is a pilgrimage that may lead us far from what we once knew as home. But we must hurry if we are to keep up with Him who is already striding across this new landscape, and who is already anticipating yet another "mission accomplished" celebration with friends and neighbours.

4. New Experiences Of Conversion

At this point in our journey we meet four real-life pilgrims, traveling side by side at the beginning of the third millennium. It may be in the stories of lived Christian conversions that we come closest to grasping the significance of the sea-changes heaving at the moorings of the church in our time. Are these stories troubling to us? Do they fit our models of Christian conversion? To some they will seem commonplace.

And yet here in these personal narratives Holy God is at work and we do well to take off our shoes. Let us go back again to our sacred text and see if we do not find these stories written there after all. Let us listen much and watch well as we respond to God's call to be partners with him in this new and foreign land.

a) The Grace Of Conversion As Process

Emily[103] was born into a committed Pentecostal family, and was swept up into the life of the church—Sunday School, choir, youth group. In her early teens she was baptized. To all appearances she was tracking well. But then, as she got older,

---

[103] These, of course, are not the real names.

her tidy religious world refused to be held together, and she walked away from the church and away from God.

What happened during those wilderness years? When she knows us better she may say more—we don't need to be over-curious. But now, at 47 she is confident, capable, and reconnecting with God. Emily is sympathetic towards other religions in a way that would make her childhood mentors squeamish, but she has concluded that she will best know God through Jesus.

For thus says the LORD:
When seventy years
are completed for Babylon,
I will visit you, and
I will fulfill to you my promise
and bring you back to this place.
For I know the plans
I have for you,
declares the LORD,
plans for welfare and not for evil,
to give you a future and a hope.
Then you will call upon me and
come and pray to me,
and I will hear you.
You will seek me and find me,
when you seek me with
all your heart.
Jeremiah 29:10-13

She ventured quietly into the back of our traditional looking church sanctuary to find herself in the midst of a diversity unimaginable to her childhood, but richly appealing. When she attended the membership class she said, "I knew if I was going to grow spiritually I had to be involved in a Christian community."

Emily is experiencing conversion as a process. It began at an early age, but perhaps because her church and family life were so enmeshed it was difficult for her to be converted as her own person. Gordon Smith argues that only adults can be fully converted because of the complexity and depth of the conversion experience. He even says that for some people, the only way they can be fully converted is to leave the church![104]

There was good that came out of Emily's time away. She has had an extended period of differentiation from family and church, and perhaps from God. Though we remember that God is always nearer and more active in the wilderness than we suspect. And now she is resuming the journey as a mature adult.

We did not ask Emily to be re-baptized. Her early baptism stands as a valid component of her protracted conversion. We acknowledge and appreciate her journey. At this point it is clear that her eyes are turned to Jesus (think "centred set model"). And there is no doubt she is far enough along the journey to satisfy the boundary crossing requirements of membership in a Baptist church. Though it is plain that for Emily, membership is not about institutional loyalty, it is about a relational commitment.

Emily is experiencing the grace of conversion as process. Furthermore, she recognizes the importance of the community in all this. She has a new appreciation for the life, the worship, even the physical space of church. She is served by the continuity of the church (that was still there for her when it was time to return.) She recognizes that her personal pilgrimage is linked to the church's corporate pilgrimage. And she in turn is important to this community. Emily's presence challenges us to grow relationally, to become a more authentic community. Her life with God reminds us that He is not rushed.

May we resist the temptation to constrain others to our conversion model. May we listen and learn and partner with

---

[104] Gordon Smith, p. 213.

God in his converting, remembering that wherever we go and whenever we speak, he has been there before us.

b) The Grace Of Conversion As Event

The intercom rang, "A Mr. Li is on the phone. He says he needs to become a Christian *today*. He wants to know if one of the pastors could come and see him." As I drive through traffic I try to prepare for what might lie ahead. I barely know this man. He and his wife regularly come to the English service but they don't stay for coffee. I thought he was already a Christian.

I would soon get to know them both much better.

Mr. and Mrs. Li came as unwilling exiles to Canada from India in the sixties, during a time of tension between India and China. They were allowed to take only what would fit in two suitcases. But they worked hard and did well in their strange new land. They have four children and a number of grandchildren.

Mrs. Li had been converted to Christ in India. Mr. Li didn't protest, he even accompanied her to church, but he refused to follow Jesus. He had his own religion. In his office was a small idol and some sticks of incense and a little mechanical device to help him pray. He worshiped before his idol every morning.

Seek the LORD
while he may be found;
call upon him while he is near;
let the wicked forsake
his way,
and the unrighteous man
his thoughts;
let him return to the LORD,
that he may have
compassion on him,
and to our God,
for he will
abundantly pardon.

Isaiah 55:6, 7

But the previous night Mr. Li had a disturbing dream. In the dream God told him that he had resisted Christ long enough. If he did not repent on the following day it would be too late. And he had taken the warning to heart.

So there we sat at the kitchen table where I read a few appropriate Scriptures. But it was hardly necessary. He knew what he needed to know from years of being in church alongside his wife. It was not more information he needed, but a decision. And he was now ready to make that decision. My role seemed almost insignificant. I simply invited him to pray with me. It was as though I opened the gate, and he walked into the Kingdom.

Ever the skeptic, I wondered how deep this was going. Can conversion be so simple? But over the next weeks and months, family and friends talked about the transformation. In fact the change was evident from that first afternoon.

"What shall I do with the idol?" he asked me.

"What would you like to do with it?" I countered.

"I just want to get rid of it," he replied.

So we scooped everything into a cardboard box and I put it into the back of the van. Not having my *Baptist Manual for Worship and Service* with me I improvised and simply tossed the idol into the dumpster behind the co-op supermarket on the way home.

When Mr. Li was baptized a few months later a whole pew full of friends and former co-workers came to see. Mr. Li was about 75 years of age at the time.

As we rediscover the grace of conversion as process we must not forget the grace of conversion as event. People growing up in Christendom (here colonial Christendom) may need to be urged to make a decision. In this case God dialed him up directly, but often he will speak through us. One woman, long a part of the church, said as I asked her if she wanted to be baptized, "No one ever asked me before." I was stunned.

A dateable of decision may also be important for people with no Christian background who are drawn into the life of the church. Many immigrants from China are first converted to the community, then later converted to the Lord of the community. They have a whole new view of the universe to absorb. After a couple of years, they are now ready to respond to a gentle challenge to cross over. Baptism often becomes for them the focal point of conversion, and the willingness to be baptized indicates the turning of the heart.

For people who grew up in a decision-addicted environment the discovery of conversion as a process is liberating. But there is still a time and place for helping people "drive a stake in the ground" to underscore the event-ness of conversion. Gibbs rightly observes that the call for a new birth is often subdued in over-reaction to "decisionism."[105]

In modernity, individuality was idolized; whereas in these post-modern times the importance of the community, the tribe, is once again seen and felt. Where is the balance? Conversion as event, and the role of decision in that event, relates to the individuality of human beings. It takes an individual to make a decision, and the community life of the church cannot be meaningful without a strong appreciation of the individuality of each member.

---

[105] Gibbs 2000, p. 89.

The balance between community and individuality is closely related to the balance between conversion as process, and conversion as event. The environment of post-modernity is helping us recover that balance.

c) The Concern For Authentic Conversion

Greg first came to church on a bright summer Sunday morning. He came in a wheel chair. His disease was advancing and he was no longer able to walk more than a few steps. He came because his caregiver wanted him to be saved, and time seemed to be running out. In the providence of God it happened that they came as I was beginning a series of sermons on Job. This classic story of one man's desperate wrestling with God seemed to touch Greg's heart. They stayed.

Greg had some experience of church life when he was a child. But since then he had been disconnected. Greg was very successful in business and had traveled widely. His marriage had not lasted, but he had a beautiful young daughter. Now this degenerative disease was turning his life in a new and unwelcome direction. Yet it was also turning his heart towards God. He was well aware he would not be thinking so much about God if he were not so seriously ill.

Greg enjoyed the warmth of the church community. He is a likeable person and loved by everyone. He made a point of attending classes and events other than Sunday worship—no small feat for him in his condition. Then a man who had taken Greg under his wing suggested he be baptized. I invited him to the baptism classes and he came.

Prior to baptism all candidates in our church were interviewed by two deacons to confirm (hopefully) their readiness for baptism. As it turned out the men who interviewed Greg were disturbed to find that "Greg had never invited Jesus into his heart." After sharing some Scripture verses with him and explaining the plan of salvation they led him in the sinners' prayer.

Greg expressed appreciation for their concern, though later he referred, with a grin, to his "inquisition." Greg was baptized (in his case, of necessity, by sprinkling) with the rest of the baptism candidates. The two deacons, however, were deeply concerned that I would allow someone to come to the point of baptism without having experienced (to use my words) conversion as an event.

For one of the men this precipitated a crisis in his relationship with the church. Was this a liberal church? Did we allow nominal Christians to be baptized and enter the church? I tried to share my thoughts on conversion as both event and process. But I was not able to allay his concern. This incident tested our friendship.

The issue here is the question of authenticity. How do we know someone is a real Christian? My friend and I both desire to see a church of authentic believers. The question is, how can we be confident of that? For my friend, to be authentic, a conversion must involve a prescribed event, specifically "inviting Jesus into your heart." I am less convinced that such an event (or any other event) guarantees authenticity. I feel more confident looking for evidence over time.

Neither is my friend comfortable about seeing baptism as the primary conversion marker. He said it feels like

Catholicism. For my part, I believe that baptism is a powerful sign of Christian conversion, especially in this post-Christendom era. Is baptism not the conversion marker prescribed in the Great Commission?

In Greg's case I was glad to see him moving forward in faith. At the time I felt that baptism would be a means of grace to move him further, while to delay baptism might stall the movement. My "centred set" approach to the spiritual pilgrimage means that if I sense movement in the right direction I am comfortable with ambiguity about boundary crossing. A number of years later I was glad to hear that Greg was still pressing forward in his relationship with the Lord and finding even deeper levels of assurance and grace.

Now when they heard this they were cut to the heart, and said to Peter and the rest of the apostles, "Brothers, what shall we do?" And Peter said to them, "Repent and be baptized every one of you in the name of Jesus Christ for the forgiveness of your sins, and you will receive the gift of the Holy Spirit.

. . .

So those who received his word were baptized, and there were added that day about three thousand souls.

Acts 2:37, 38, 41

Nevertheless, I recognize that I am by nature non-confrontational. I tend to back away from precipitating an "event." So this discussion pushed me to compensate for my natural tendencies by deliberately looking for opportunities to call for a decision that I might otherwise have missed.

This case also illustrates another aspect of the amazing diversity of the church of the third millennium—it's theological diversity. For most of those deacons, the nature of

Greg's pilgrimage would not have raised concern (they would have concerns in other areas!) The challenge for me as pastor was to find a place of rest in the midst of such diversity. The church is not a tidy place. But I am not called to tidy up what God is doing. I must be ready to allow God to continue my own conversion, and at the same time be a brother to others who are wrestling with their ongoing conversion.

d) Pressing On Toward the Goal

Bill stands at the door, holding his wife's hand, waiting for the next person to hug. Not many escape. At 92 you can get away with hugging almost everyone. For middle-aged Chinese women, unused to demonstrating affection in public, the hug comes as a bit of a shock—but they get accustomed to it and wait in line.

Twenty years earlier Bill had already been long retired from his position as school principle. But then came the opportunity to teach English as a second language to newcomers in the church setting. And with his first class he was hooked. Bill was a gifted motivator and organizer. He grew the program until we maxed out every possible classroom space with up to 300 students.

It was a remarkable ministry, not least because of his emphasis on prayer. For Bill, nothing happened without prayer. Until he was sidelined by ill health he joined me in my office for prayer at least four mornings a week.

Bill saw ESL as an opportunity to share his faith and he used the Bible to teach English. He and his wife offered extra Bible classes when the ESL program was not running. He patiently introduced his students to the Christian story. And he didn't mind if it took time. He said of one student, "He still calls himself a Buddhist. But he reads the Bible every day and when he prays he prays to Jesus." Bill could live with that. He was willing to wait on the Lord for the day his new friend would be brought all the way home.

Bill often shared with me his latest discoveries of faith. He read extensively. He continued to grow. He was still being transformed as he passed away in his 95th year.

Conversion is not an end in itself. The goal of conversion is transformation. We are being transformed into the likeness of Christ (2 Corinthians 3:18 again). A healthy church is a community of transforming people. The community itself is being transformed even as it nurtures the transformation of its members. As we have seen above, Smith argues persuasively that the quality of our *transformation* depends on the quality of our *conversion*. He urges

> *And I am sure of this,*
> *that he who began*
> *a good work in you*
> *will bring it to completion*
> *at the day of Jesus Christ.*
>
> Philippians 1:6

the church to engender more holistic conversions and so provide a better foundation for substantive transformations.

How serious are we about the goal of conversion? If our strategy is to maximize the number of *conversions* we will be content with minimalist conversions. But if our strategy is to maximize the number of *transformations* we will strive for more thorough conversions.

May we so lift up Christ in the church that those who come (and we ourselves) may be so drawn to him that they not only cross a border (important though that is) but are drawn ever deeper, year by year, into the heart and home of our Triune God.

Conclusion

This is not the time for hard and fast conclusions about conversion. Tomorrow will bring new and unforeseen sets of circumstances that will raise new crops of questions. But thus far we can say this: *we must still be born again.* And perhaps we are now in a better position to understand the momentous reality of being born again than we have been for some time.

Under Christendom we didn't really need to be born again—we were all Christians anyway. Under modernity if we were born again it had to be done privately: at that time of the day who, out on the street, was going to take supernatural issues seriously? Under the pervasive influence of the Boomers we didn't need to be born again, we were still seeking the full potential of our first birth. Under the illusion of a monocultural world, if we were born again we knew exactly what that would look like, we were reborn into our own culture. In the liberal world we were all so nice we didn't need to be born again. In the fundamentalist/revivalist world it was so critical that we be born again that we were date-stamped.

But now in this strange new land of the third millennium, conversion is much more sharply defined. The lines between Christian and non-Christian are much more clearly drawn. Against the backdrop of the New Barbarian the radical nature of Christian conversion is thrown into severe relief. To follow Jesus is once again a salty, life-threatening adventure.

GenXers and Millennials who consider crossing over have no interest in going for a paddle. They want nothing less than a full immersion conversion that transforms the way they feel and taste and touch, as well as the way they think and relate and live. They resonate with the raw faith of the early church. And in this post-modern environment they have been released to draw on that rich historical heritage.

As the arguing settles somewhat between the liberals and fundamentalists we are able to hear a range of overtones in conversion we had missed earlier—the mystery, the sense of journey, the wonder that God should love me, the awe of realizing that the Lord is in this place and we were not aware of him, that conversion is first of all God initiated.

Now, as not before in recent years, we have the privilege of experiencing such a depth of conversion that it might actually be like being "born again." Perhaps now it is again possible to be "born again"!

We, the people of God, have a story to tell, a Glorious, Grand Narrative. Though they may not yet realize it the new pilgrims are hungry for this Gospel, and now is the time to declare it. Let us do so with Christian boldness, which is not arrogance but the confident assurance that is the birthright of the children of God. Let this be a corporate boldness, a story spoken and lived out, in and from the life of the community of the followers of Jesus, as we model together God's good future for our neighbours.

So as we venture into the uncharted waters of the third millennium we have a marvelous opportunity to relearn what it means to be co-workers with God as he orchestrates the conversion of a new generation. Yes, pastoral work is now much more complex, much messier. We still serve people shaped by Christendom and modernity, and we must not neglect them. But we also serve people who are natives of a very different land, to whom Christendom, modernity, monoculture, liberalism and fundamentalism, are foreign concepts.

How good it is to remember that Jesus remains the Captain of our salvation (Hebrews 2:10), the Author and Perfecter of our faith (Hebrews 12:2). This present age has not caught him by surprise. Indeed, we are now in a position to appreciate even more deeply the richness of his Great Commission that speaks to us with even greater urgency and relevance at the beginning of the third millennium.

Jesus came
and said to them,

"All authority in heaven and on earth
has been given to me.

Go therefore
and make disciples
of all nations,

baptizing them
in the name of
the Father and of the Son and of the Holy Spirit,

teaching them
to observe
all that I have commanded you.

And behold,
I am with you always,
to the end of the age."

Matthew 28:18-20

The Great Commission
Third Millennium Reflections

Jesus came

Jesus is not lying dead in that stone tomb, he is resurrected, he is alive! And this changes everything. The Great Commission is bracketed by the living presence of Jesus, Immanuel, God with us. Jesus is all over this assignment. No mission happens apart from him. He is the first and greatest missionary, sent out from heaven to earth. All others are never more than apprentice missionaries. He is the initiater, shaper, sustainer, and finisher of the task. This remains true in our present complex times also. He is just as much at home in our strange new world as he was in New Testament Palestine.

Notice also who Jesus came to—both worshipers *and* doubters (see verse 17). This is so encouraging in our post-modern world when "bomb-proof certainty" is in such short supply. There is room in the heart of Jesus for the weary, the wary, and the cynical. And there's room in the Great Commission also. From the beginning Jesus has been commissioning less-than-perfect individuals and communities. Does this assignment seem over our heads? Welcome to the club! We are reminded that, "we have this treasure in jars of clay, to show that the surpassing power belongs to God and not to us" (2 Corinthians 4:7). To God be the glory.

and said to them,

Praise God, we are not left to wonder what Jesus has in mind for us as he prepares to depart (physically) this world. He *speaks*. And his famous last words have been written into the inspired text. In this time of constant flux and shape-shifting landscape, when everything is "on the table" and open to question, and we must check the compass every morning, how good it is to have the words of Jesus in writing. Our assignment is that clear.

There are those within the church who want to redefine the assignment. They rightly remember that Jesus went about doing good. And doing good is much less offensive to our suspicious neighbours than making disciples of Jesus. And surely the need for doing good is greater than ever. But who will make disciples of Jesus if the followers of Jesus do not? Have we forgotten his famous last words? Whatever other good we may also engage in, may this commission take priority.

We notice, also, that Jesus speaks to "*them.*" How often have we heard and felt the Great Commission as a solo endeavour. But this is a *corporate* assignment, the verbs are all second person *plural* ("y'all go and make disciples, y'all baptize them and teach them!") What a weight this lifts off our shoulders! As a church, as a community, as a team, we engage in the task *together*, each contributing her or his gift. One shares, one talks, one listens, one invites, one challenges, one smiles, one embraces . . . Together we embody our Lord Christ to the surprise and delight of our lonely neighbours. Amazingly, surprisingly, miraculously, the church becomes an evangelistic presence in our post-modern, post-Christendom neighbourhoods. And by God's grace, disciples are birthed.

"All authority in heaven and on earth has been given to me.

We are nervous about Christian mission. We think it is a dodgy, fragile, misguided, ill-advised venture, especially in our current, minority-status environment. We are intimidated by the chorus of voices telling us to be silent, challenging our right to even talk about Jesus.

But the truth is that we have more right to tell the Gospel than anyone else has to forbid us. No Muslim or Hindu, certainly no strident secularist, is more authorized than we are.

The Father has given Jesus a "name that is above every name" (Philippians 2:9). He has put everything "in subjection under his feet" (Hebrews 2:8). If Jesus were no more than a wise teacher, or an above average prophet, then we have problems, we are right to be nervous. But Jesus is Lord of heaven and earth. Whom then shall we fear! Do we fear satan?—he is a crushed enemy. Do we fear death?—"Death is swallowed up in victory!" (1 Corinthians 15:55).

The church is commissioned by him who has *all* authority, not limited or partial authority, not just authority within our own tribe. There is not one square yard of this planet that is not under his authority. How this frees us to obey. There is no dark corner of our world or neighbourhood where we are not under the umbrella of his authority.

And we, too, are under his authority. These strong words are not just for our comfort out in the new "multi-verse." This is a word to our own wandering, reluctant hearts. "Listen up! This is the Boss speaking!" With him all things are possible. We remember his confident words: "I will build my church, and the gates of hell shall not prevail against it" (Matthew 16:18). The Great Commissioner will fulfill his dreams.

Go therefore

"Go" . . . there is always this outward movement in mission. There is no mission without a "going" of some kind, even if only across the hall. Thus the words "apostle" (from Greek *apostellein*, "to send") and "missionary" (from Latin *missio*, "mission" and *mittere*, "to send"). We are the "sent ones."

Technically the Greek word behind "go" is a participle, not an imperative. A stricter translation might be "going," which could be read as, "when you go," or "as you go." The common translation "go" is justifiable, since a participle followed by an imperative can take the sense of that following imperative (see Matthew 28:7 for a similar construction). But does not this grammatical detail hint at our *reluctance* to go? Thus the Great Commission begins more with prophecy than command. Jesus tells us, "As you go (because I will see to it that you *do* go!) make disciples." We remember how the early believers had to be driven out of their comfortable homes in Jerusalem (Acts 8:1).

So often in history, and perhaps no more so than in our present day, the salvation of the human race seems to hang by a very weak human thread (childless Abraham, irresolute Isaac, cheating Jacob, and so on.) But if we peer behind the scenes, there is God at work, lovingly, but unstoppably, bringing his plans to completion. Our "going" takes us from the known, comfortable, secure place, into the unknown, uncertain place— a post-modern, post-Christendom, multi-tribal world. Of course we will kick back. Maintenance is much more comfortable than mission. But we will go. We will discover that our weak wills are eclipsed by the vigorous will of God himself. And we will learn to delight in the expedition.

and make disciples

The command is not merely to populate heaven (to get people saved "by the skin of their teeth"), nor merely to accumulate church members here below, but to make *disciples of Jesus.* That is, to lead people into thorough Christian conversions, evidenced by deep inner and outer transformation. What a wide range of skills and abilities this calls for. To disciple is to mentor, to apprentice, to teach by example, to invite someone to live alongside us (as Jesus did) and to follow in our footsteps. Who dare take on this work? It eases the weight to remember that this is a *corporate* assignment. We are called to be a disciple-making community.

We *will* make disciples, simply by being in this world. We *will* influence people. There will always be those who walk in our footsteps (friends, colleagues, students, grandchildren). The question is what kind of disciples will they be? We should not complain about the disciples we end up with. We get the disciples we deserve.

So Jesus calls us to be intentional about our disciple-making, and to follow in the footsteps of *his* disciple-making. What a commitment! He went to them, he called them, he lived with them, he ate with them, he taught them, he opened his heart to them, he wept and prayed and preached in front of them, year after year after year. Do we ever graduate from the school of discipleship?—never! There are aspects of discipleship that can only be learned in old age.

Christian disciples are those whose hearts are drawn into alignment with the heart of Jesus. This is a consuming relationship that redraws their map of their universe and rescripts every aspect of their belief and behaviour.

of all nations,

This answers the "who?" question (just in case we are thinking this only applies to people like us!) Why do we still have so many mono-cultural churches?—White churches, Black churches, Korean churches, Estonian churches . . . . Perhaps, for a while, they help new immigrants, challenged with language and culture, get a foot in the door. But still homogenious after three generations . . . ?

The Greek word is *ethne*, reminding us to be careful to make disciples, not just of all nation states, but of all ethnic groups within all nation states. (French Canadians are the largest unreached people-group in North America.) In our post-monocultural world it is not difficult to make a start. Even small-town churches now have the opportunity to model the new and living temple built of men and women from every nation with Jesus as the chief cornerstone (Ephesians 2:11-22).

Every church can have appropriate foreign-language Bibles on hand. Why would the Lord send a minority-group seeker to a church that is unprepared? What does the welcome mat look like in my church? Is the word "WELCOME" written in English only? Do we sing songs written by older white Anglos only? Are we willing to "go" linguistically and culturally, as well as geographically?

We have often resisted the "of all nations" part of the Great Commission. The people of God are not immune to xenophobia, as the Bible illustrates all too well. This was a major hurdle to be crossed in the early church (read Acts 10f.) But, as a friend of mine likes to say, "Once you've worshiped in colour, you'll never go back to black and white." (And the pot-luck dinners are fabulous!)

baptizing them

Now we get to the "how?" of making disciples: part a) "baptizing them." Not forced baptisms surely, but leading people to the place where they are ready for baptism.

Some, the remnant children of Christendom, are very close, sitting on the edge of the baptistry, so to speak, needing only a little push. They've grown up with the Gospel, they are already immersed in Christian values and worldview. The watery immersion will be their confession of personal faith and their formal initiation into the family of God.

But others in our post-Christian environment are far from the baptistry. They are not even aware they have just walked past a church building. Such structures are not flagged on their world map. They are immersed in very different belief systems. Their theology (we all have one) may be an eclectic, unexamined mix, absorbed from popular culture. Or it may be aligned with one of the countless tribal theologies readily available in our new, inter-connected world. But in God's mercy these good folk also encounter the tribe of Christ.

Who is the star soul-winner in these conversions? More than likely, in our day, it will be the church as a whole, under the gracious choreography of the Holy Spirit, who brings the new pilgrims home. Over the next five years, over countless cups of coffee, and through numerous interactions in homes and schools and marketplace, with diverse members of the Christian community, they too are brought to the cusp, ready to plunge into a radically new world.

They will be baptized, not because it is the thing to do, nor to please their parents. Their baptism will be their manifesto, their declaration of allegiance and obedience to Christ alone.

in the name of the Father and of the Son and of the Holy Spirit,

And let us give them a fully *Christian* baptism. Crisp definitions are so helpful at the beginning of the third millennium. This is not a conversion to western culture. This is not a conversion to undefined spirituality (candles, robes, and generic prayers, more quiet music, and less red meat.) This is not a conversion to Judaism or Islam. This is a conversion to a robust, Trinitarian Christianity.

We baptize them *"into"* (Gk. *eis*) the name, the reality, of the Father, Son, and Holy Spirit. They are immersed into a whole new *understanding* of life based on the Trinitarian nature of God. But even more than that, they are immersed into the *relational* life of the Father, Son, and Holy Spirit.

To be a disciple of Jesus is, at the same time, to be a disciple of the Father and the Spirit. We do not have three gods but One. The persons of the Trinity are so intimately connected that to have a relationship with one is to have a relationship with all. Jesus, the man from Galilee, incarnate in human flesh and bones, brings us to the throne room of Holy God and the very heart of the Father. And the Holy Spirit is an equal partner. Baptism marks the beginning of our walk in and with the Spirit.

Baptism, like a wedding, signals both a leaving as well as a cleaving. This new relationship with the Father, Son, and Spirit is so intimate and encompassing, as with marriage, that all other calls must take second place.

Welcome to the family of God! A seat has been reserved for you. How good this is for the fractured, lonely, lost wanderers of our times.

teaching them to observe all that I have commanded you.

"Teaching them what?" we ask. And Matthew answers, "How about reading my disciple-makers' handbook!" This Gospel appears to have been shaped, from the beginning, with the closing Great Commission in mind. Matthew has given us a memorable, narrative, pocket theology. He has conveniently arranged the teachings of Jesus into five, easy-to-remember blocks. He has rooted his Gospel firmly in the Jewish past, but he also throws out the welcome mat for Gentiles. Prediction: In our post-Christendom, mission-hearted churches Matthew's Gospel will once again become the most popular of the four. It was so in the early days of the church.

So how do we turn our neo-pagan neighbours into disciples?—by a) "baptizing them," and b) "teaching them." But note again the depth of conversion Jesus has in mind. This teaching is not to be simply "information transfer." They are to *observe*, to *put into practice*, the commands of Jesus.

Notice that we are not told to teach the *unbaptized* to observe the commands of Jesus. Only those who are serious about crossing over to Jesus' camp will tolerate the heavy medicine of such requirements as "love your enemies," and "take up your cross." Only those immersed in the Spirit can seriously expect to bear the fruit of a transformed character.

Strikingly, it is not the law of Moses we are to teach, but "all that I [Jesus] have commanded you." From anyone else, what arrogance! But from Jesus, so right, so good. The words of Jesus are to shape our hearing of all other words (even the words of Moses).

So how are we doing in our *own* training regimen? Is our age appropriate to our discipleship grade?

And behold, I am with you always, to the end of the age"

How are the eleven feeling about their assignment at this point? "You've got to be kidding! We are inadequate, unstable, depressed, doubting sinners." Do we ever feel this way?

Then comes this remarkable promise of the presence of the resurrected Jesus "always, to the end of the age," including through these present, choppy, uncharted waters at the start of the third millennium. It calls to mind the words of the Psalm:

> If I take the wings of the morning
> and dwell in the uttermost parts of the sea,
> even there your hand shall lead me,
> and your right hand shall hold me (Psalm 139: 9,10).

O Joy! What comfort! What motivation! What freedom to obey to the uttermost!

We are not still trying to weasel out of this assignment are we?—as in: "Jesus was talking to them not me"? But surely if the *promise* extends through 2000 years to the present and beyond, does the *command* not extend as far? Dare we claim the promise if we don't obey the command? Listen, beloved of the Lord, we also are invited, no, *commissioned*, to share in the joy of the Lord in his outpouring of grace in our generation.

And so the *authority* of Jesus announced earlier, and the *presence* of Jesus promised here, together underwrite the success of the mission. Now we know how Jesus could be so confident, "Follow me, and I will make you fishers of men" (Matthew 4:19). And how the harvest has poured in! All the families of the earth are being blessed, as the Lord promised to father Abraham (Genesis 12:3). And we too, as faithful co-workers with God, will carry home our share of the harvest, in our own generation.

Postscript

(Nicodemus walks in the light)

³⁸After these things Joseph of Arimathea, who was a disciple of Jesus, but secretly for fear of the Jews, asked Pilate that he might take away the body of Jesus, and Pilate gave him permission. So he came and took away his body. ³⁹Nicodemus also, who earlier had come to Jesus by night, came bringing a mixture of myrrh and aloes, about seventy-five pounds in weight. ⁴⁰So they took the body of Jesus and bound it in linen cloths with the spices, as is the burial custom of the Jews. ⁴¹Now in the place where he was crucified there was a garden, and in the garden a new tomb in which no one had yet been laid. ⁴²So because of the Jewish day of Preparation, since the tomb was close at hand, they laid Jesus there.

John 19:38-42

Bibliography

Beaudoin, Tom. *Virtual Faith: The Irreverent Spiritual Quest of Generation X.* San Francisco, CA: Jossey-Bass, 1998.

Bebbington, David W. *Evangelicalism in Modern Britain: A History From the 1730s to the 1980s.* Routledge: 1989.

Berger, Peter L. *The Sacred Canopy: Elements of a Sociological Theory of Religion.* New York, NY: Doubleday Anchor, 1969.

Clapp, Rodney. *A Peculiar People: The Church As Culture In A Post-Christian Society.* Downers Grove, IL: InterVarsity Press, 1996.

Coote, Robert T. and John Stott eds. *Down To Earth: Studies In Christianity and Culture.* Grand Rapids, MI: Eerdmans, 1980.

Dockery, David S. ed. *The Challenge of Postmodernism: An Evangelical Engagement.* Grand Rapids, MI: Baker, 2nd ed. 2001.

Engel, James F. and Wilbert Norton. *What's Gone Wrong With the Harvest?: A Communication Strategy for the Church and World.* Zondervan, 1975.

Erickson, Millard J. *Truth Or Consequences: The Promise & Perils of Postmodernism.* Downers Grove, IL: InterVarsity Press, 2001.

Flory, Richard W. and Donald E. Miller eds. *GenX Religion.* New York, NY: Routledge, 2000.

Forrester, John A. *Grace for Shame: The Forgotten Gospel.* Pastor's Attic Press, 2014.

Frank, Thomas E.. *The Soul of the Congregation: An Invitation to Congregational Reflection.* Nashville, TN: Abingdon, 2000.

Gibbs, Eddie and Ian Coffey. *Church Next: Quantum Changes in Christian Ministry.* Leicester, UK: InterVarsity, 2001.

Gibbs, Eddie. *In Name Only: Tackling The Problem Of Nominal Christianity.* Pasadena, CA: Fuller, 2000 ed.

Guder, Darrell L. ed. *Missional Church: A Vision for the Sending of the Church in North America.* Grand Rapids, MI: Eerdmans, 1998.

Guinness, Os. *Dining With The Devil: The Megachurch Movement Flirts With Modernity.* Grand Rapids, MI: Baker, 1993.

Gundry, Robert H. *Mark: A Commentary On His Apology For The Cross.* Grand Rapids, MI: Eerdmans, 1992.

Hunter III, George G. *The Celtic Way of Evangelism: How Christianity Can Reach the West . . . Again.* Nashville, TN: Abingdon, 2001.

Hunter III, George G. *Church For The Unchurched.* Nashville, TN: Abingdon, 1996.

Jenkins, Philip. "The Next Christianity." *Atlantic Monthly,* October 2002.

Kew, Richard. *Brave New Church: What The Future Holds.* Harrisburg, PA: Morehouse, 2001.

McGrath, Alister E. *The Future of Christianity.* Malden, MA: Blackwell, 2002.

Mead, Loren B. *The Once And Future Church: Reinventing The Congregation For A New Mission Frontier.* The Alban Institute, 1992 ed.

Oden, Thomas C. *After Modernity . . . What?* Grand Rapids, MI: Zondervan, 1990.

Peace, Richard. *Conversion in the New Testament: Paul and the Twelve.* Grand Rapids, MI: Eerdmans, 1999.

Regele, Mike. *Death of the Church.* Grand Rapids, MI: Zondervan, 1995.

Roof, Wade Clark. *Spiritual Marketplace: Baby Boomers and the Remaking of American Religion*. Princeton, NJ: Princeton UP, 1999.

Roxburgh, Alan J. *The Missionary Congregation, Leadership, & Liminality*. Harrisburg, PA: Trinity Press International, 1997.

Schaller, Lyle E. *Discontinuity & Hope: Radical Change and the Path to the Future*. Nashville, TN: Abingdon, 1999.

Schaller, Lyle E. *The New Reformation: Tomorrow Arrived Yesterday*. Nashville, TN: Abingdon, 1995.

Smith, Chuck. *The End of the World As We Know It: Clear Directions For Bold and Innovative Ministry In a Postmodern World*. Colorado Springs, CO: WaterBrook, 2001.

Smith, Gordon T. *Beginning Well: Christian Conversion & Authentic Transformation*. Downers Grove, IL: InterVarsity, 2001.

Sweet, Leonard. *AquaChurch*. Loveland, CO: Group, 1999.

Webber, Robert. *Ancient-Future Faith: Rethinking Evangelicalism for a Postmodern World*. Grand Rapids, MI: Baker, 1999.

Webber, Robert. *Journey to Jesus: The Worship, Evangelism and Nurture Mission of the Church*. Nashville, TN: Abingdon, 2001.

Zimmerman, John C. "Leadership Across the Gaps Between Generations." *Crux* 31, no. 2 (June 1995).

www.ingramcontent.com/pod-product-compliance
Lightning Source LLC
Chambersburg PA
CBHW060513030426
42337CB00015B/1872